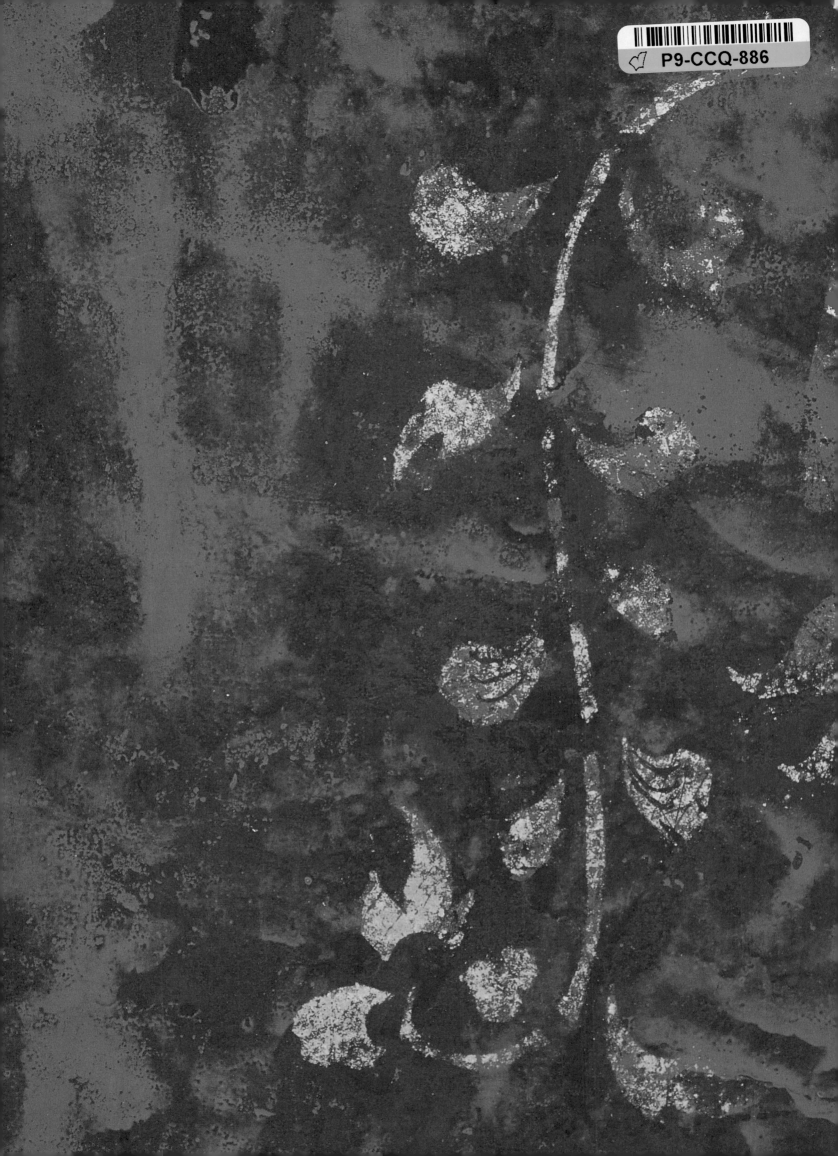

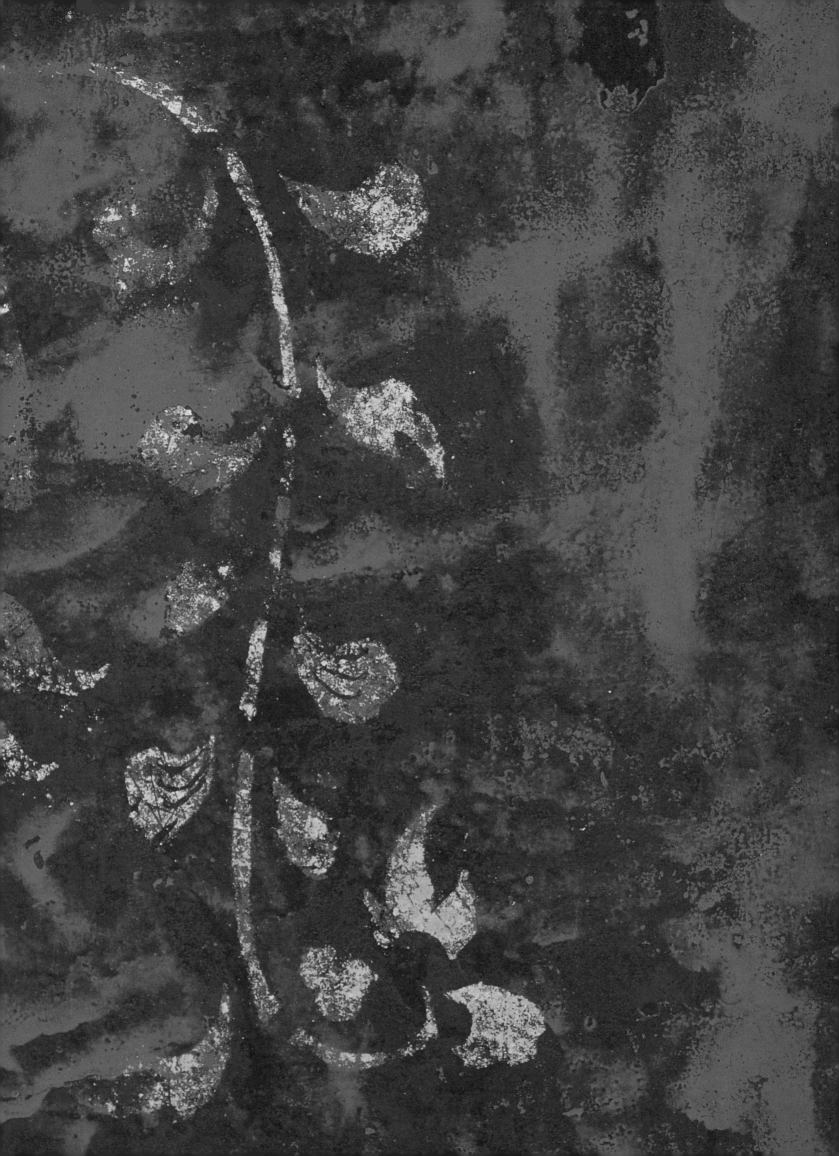

Tropical
Asian
Style

TROPICAL
INTERIORS

Tropical
Asian
Style

Concept, styling and photography: Luca Invernizzi Tettoni
Editing: Kim Inglis
Design: William Atyeo
Text: Gianni Francione, Madé Wijaya, Robert Powell,
Julian Davison, Diana Darling, William Warren,
Nigel Simmonds, Lawrence Blair, Bruce W Carpenter,
Leonard Lueras, Kim Inglis, Carole Muller, Edric Ong,
David Wiles, Teresa Woods-Hunt, David Sinclair
and Daniel Kahrs.

PERIPLUS

EDITIONS

Published by Periplus Editions (HK) Ltd

Copyright © 1997 Periplus Editions (HK) Ltd
ALL RIGHTS RESERVED
ISBN 962-593-136-8
Printed in Singapore

Publisher: Eric Oey
Associate Publisher: Christina Ong
Editor: Kim Inglis
Design: William Atyeo

Distributors:
Australia: Bookwise International,
54 Crittenden Rd., Findon SA 5023
Indonesia: P.T. Wira Mandala Pustaka
(Java Books – Indonesia), Jl Kelapa Gading Kirana,
Blok A-14 No. 17, Jakarta 14240
New Zealand: Nationwide Book Distributors Ltd.,
PO Box 4176, Christchurch
Singapore & Malaysia: Berkeley Books Pte. Ltd.,
5 Little Road #08-01, Singapore 536983
Thailand: Asia Books Co. Ltd.,
5 Sukhumvit Soi 61, Bangkok 10110
USA: Charles E. Tuttle Co. Inc., RRI Box 231-5,
North Clarendon, VT 05759-9700

CONTENTS

The modern Asian house—interpreted and adapted—encourages a close relationship with the surrounding tropical environment.

THE TROPICAL HOUSE

Introduction

Toward the end of the 1920s, along the sun-dappled southern coast of the island then known as Ceylon, a European aristocrat experienced a moment of intense personal revelation. It was not Count de Mauny-Talvande's first trip to Ceylon. That had been in 1912, when he came as a guest of Sir Thomas Lipton, the tea magnate, and fell in love with the languid tropical atmosphere.

After this visit, some time during the First World War, something terrible happened to the Count. Exactly what is unclear, but its effects were sufficient to make him abandon Europe, return to the East, and embark on a restless search for what he called "one spot which, by its sublime beauty, would fulfil my dreams and hold me there for life".

It took nearly ten years before his "endless seeking Destiny" brought him to the little fishing village of Welligama, and there, just 50 yards or so offshore, rose a rocky mount covered with lush foliage: a toy island almost, the very embodiment of south-sea-island fantasies, and,

to all appearances, quite empty. The Count swam across the narrow stretch of water and climbed to the top. "I sat for a long while on a boulder overhanging the sea," he wrote later, "wishing that this island lost in the Indian Ocean were mine; picturing and planning what I should do with it. I felt my heart beating with the overwhelming desire to create, the pride of creation, and to find in it peace, the nearest thing to happiness. Yes, it would, it must, be the home which I had dreamt of so many years past."

And so it became. He changed the name from Galduwa, Singhalese for "rocky island", to Taprobane, the old Greek name for Ceylon, and then proceeded to build on it an extraordinary house. "Not a real house with an interior" according to a later resident who was similarly smitten with Taprobane, "but a pavilion which would be a continuation of the landscape outside, and from every point of which there would be multiple

PREVIOUS PAGE
A large conservatory has been added to this "black and white" house in Singapore.

OPPOSITE
Count de Mauny-Talvande, as depicted in a painting by David Paynter.

LEFT
Two old photographs of Taprobane, the Count's dream home in Sri Lanka. *Far left* shows a terrace the Count named Our Lady's Blue Garden; *near left* is the south loggia overlooking the sea.

ABOVE
The island and house of Count de Mauny-Talvande, off the coast of Sri Lanka. He—and many others like him—severed ties with their past lives, moved to Asia and constructed deeply personal "tropical dream homes".

ABOVE
The German artist Walter
Spies moved to Bali in
1927, and built a fantastic
house in the cooler climate
of Ubud. Here, with his pet
cockatoo and monkey, he
immersed himself in the
culture of the island.

views. And so, blithely, he did away with walls between the rooms so that all nine rooms (including the bathroom) would in reality be only one, and that one open to the wind. Then, having chosen as his aesthetic north a little island across the bay whose form he particularly liked, he constructed his octagonal house so that from its exact centre that island would be visible— framed first by columns, then by a further doorway, the paths of the formal garden, and finally by the hand-planted jungle beyond. The result is very rational and, like most things born of fanaticism, wildly impractical."

To the Count, it made perfect sense. "Sometimes," he observed, "the gardens are laid out to suit the house; or the house may be built to suit our ideas of a garden. The latter was my case." Over the years he created a luxuriant series of terraces linked by steep stone steps, filled with exotic trees, shrubs and creepers; and here he lived, in absolute contentment, until another war forced him to return to Europe. A few years after the Second World War, however, he died—and some surmise it was of a broken heart.

Taprobane's allure, however, continued to be potent. After the war it attracted another romantic traveller, the American writer Paul Bowles, who for a number of years

divided his time between the island and the very different landscape of North Africa; and still later, it became home to an assortment of other Western escapists, among them one described in a local newspaper as being both "a Ruritanian playboy" and a "skilled sorcerer".

Perhaps what drew such a disparate group was not only the tempting isolation, but also the fact that Count de Mauny-Talvande's design, though he took it further than many others would dare, incorporated most of the essential elements of tropical architecture. Indeed, he might be looked upon as a kind of pioneer in selecting the site for his private Eden and fashioning it into a creation that not only harmonized with the environment, but reflected his own distinctive personality.

Some of these elements are dictated by the climate, and can be found in traditional buildings that evolved long before any European influences were added. In Thailand, for instance, even the simplest houses of bamboo and nipa-palm thatch were designed to catch any passing breeze and usually had sizeable verandahs where most social activities took place. Larger wooden houses, a later develop- ment for ordinary people, followed a similar plan. They had steep roofs and deep eaves to cope with heavy rains and harsh sunlight and were

elevated from the ground for protection against floods and wild animals; the various rooms, made in prefabricated sections, were arranged around a central platform which in fact served as a large verandah, sheltered in some places by the eaves, open to the sky in others. Though more concealed within a series of private courtyards and making use of water in the form of fountains and pools, classic Balinese houses were also largely open to the gardens that grew with such abandon just outside; and the same integration of climate and lifestyle can be found in the South Seas, on the volcanic slopes of Java and along the rivers of Borneo.

Count de Mauny-Talvande was by no means the only expatriate whose quest led to a remarkable dream house in the tropics. In the 1930s Adrien Le Mayeur de Merpres, a Belgian aristocrat and artist, created a famous house and statue-filled garden overlooking the sea at Sanur in Bali. On the same magical island but overlooking a dramatic ravine near Ubud, the painter Walter Spies *(above)* built a multi-level bamboo

structure that became the meeting place for visiting celebrities in the 1920s and 1930s. In Thailand, an American named Jim Thompson *(below)* not only revived the Thai silk industry but also aroused a new enthusiasm for traditional Thai

architecture through the spectacular example he assembled beside a Bangkok canal.

The same spirit motivates many today, as contemporary tropical houses employ both traditional and modern features to achieve their goals. On the following pages, we will explore the ways in which an assortment of owners and architects have sought to fulfil dreams as intensely personal, and occasionally as eccentric, as Count de Mauny-Talvande's idealistic vision of paradise.

Life in the tropics encourages a close relationship with the surrounding environment and, for that reason, many compounds display facilities for maximum exposure to balmy breezes and scented plants. Some have elegant *salas*, or pavilions, open on all sides, while on others there are spacious verandahs and open living quarters that seem natural extensions of the garden. The classic bungalow of Western colonial life, a term adapted from the Bengali word *bangla* and once a relatively simple structure with few adornments, has been transformed into something far more elaborate and imaginative, retaining the airy open quality so prized by stengah-sipping planters and their perspiring memsahibs but also full of surprising touches and luxurious comforts. Even the least conventional of Somerset Maugham's heroines, contemplating murder or adultery on her verandah in the vastness of a rubber plantation, might have hesitated before the exciting prospect of bathing or sleeping under a starry tropical night.

Water has become an essential part of such landscapes, appearing in the form of imaginative rock-hewn swimming pools with plants spilling over their edges, lily and lotus ponds spanned by bridges or stepping stones, and cascades that bring a soothing sound on even the sultriest day. Interior decoration is often equally striking. Count de Mauny-Talvande drew his inspiration from the culture of the country where he found his island. He had a central, domed "Hall of the Lotus" with carved panels showing lotus buds and flowers, a frieze inspired by ancient Singhalese frescoes on a white stone wall, furniture made of "the rarest Ceylon woods" and silken curtains that were drawn only at night.

As we will see in this book, others have also drawn on local arts to create a memorable atmosphere in their tropical dream houses: the rich texture of ornately carved wood and the earthy tones of terracotta and stone, textiles in subtle hues, vernacular baskets and lacquerware, statuary and ceramics and countless other artefacts that transform a living space into something at once beautiful and deeply personal.
William Warren

LEFT
Jim Thompson was best known for his revival of the Thai silk industry and his mysterious disappearance in Malaysia. Less well known, was his interest in Thai architecture and art— an interest that culminated in the construction of this fabulous Thai-style house on a Bangkok *klong*.

RIGHT
Watercolour by Stephen Little, depicting a locally-inspired house in a lush garden. Life in the tropics encourages a close relationship with the surrounding environment.

The Southeast Asian House

All of the houses appearing in this book are contemporary in design, yet share common features which transcend the mere fact of their tropical situation. This is because they are, to varying degrees, part of an ancient and common architectural tradition, one that may be called the style of the traditional Southeast Asian House.

In order to gain an understanding of today's tropical houses, it is necessary to take a look at the history of the region—both cultural and architectural. Whilst many of these contemporary buildings have modern features, such as up-to-date sanitation, electricity, high-tech kitchens and so on, they borrow numerous elements of local design. By tracing the development of Southeast Asian vernacular building traditions—and indeed it is very much a living tradition, found in countless places throughout the region—one comes to appreciate today's creations all the more.

One thing is certain: Southeast Asia has a very ancient building tradition, one that is characterized by the use of natural materials—timber, bamboo, thatch and fibre—and a post and beam method of construction. Houses are traditionally designed round a rectangular wooden framework consisting of vertical posts and horizontal tie-beams, supporting a pitched roof with gable ends. The living floor is raised off the ground on pile or stilt foundations—the former are sunk into the ground, while the latter typically rest on stone foundation slabs—and the roof ridge is often extended at either end to create outward sloping gables. The walls do not constitute part of the load-bearing structure as such, but rather consist of panels of wood, thatch or plaited bamboo laths, which are attached to the main framework; the whole ensemble is then put together without nails, using mortis and tenon joints and wooden pegs *(see page 23)*.

This, then, is the archetypal Southeast Asian house. Exceptions, where they exist, can be linked to historical circumstances. For example, the ground-built houses of Java and Bali probably arose during Indonesia's Classical Era (5th to 15th centuries) when there were close cultural contacts with India where this is the standard practice. Even in these instances, one still

LEFT
Longhouses were once a ubiquitous feature of the Bornean landscape. Raised high on pile foundations, they were literally home to an entire community. The basic pattern was everywhere the same, namely a series of family apartments arranged side by side which opened onto a gallery, or covered verandah, running the full length of the building. Much of daily life was enacted in this public space with the family only retiring to their rooms to eat and sleep.

The building shown here is a section of a Melanau long-house as reconstructed by the architect Edric Ong for the Sarawak Cultural Village near Kuching, Malaysia. Most Melanau today have embraced a contemporary lifestyle and there are no Melanau longhouses left in existence. This structure, which was constructed with reference to old photographs and other archival records, was assembled using traditional building materials including ironwood house posts, bark wall panels and nipa-palm thatch.

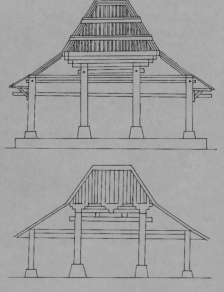

finds that the traditional rice barn in Bali is a typical Southeast Asian post and beam structure, while Classical Javanese temple reliefs (see above, Borobudur) depict house types that closely resemble contemporary stilt dwellings from northern Sumatra (see right, a Minangkabau building).

The suitability and versatility of this architectural form in relation to the environment is obvious. Because the house is raised from the ground, it affords its occupants protection from dangerous animals and the seasonal inundations

associated with living in a tropical climate. Equally importantly, the elevated living floor catches ambient breezes, whilst allowing a current of cooling air to pass beneath the floor. The gable ends of the pitched roof similarly direct breezes through the high open space, whose tunnel-like properties ventilate the house from above.

At the same time, the use of natural building materials with low thermal properties—wood, bamboo and thatch—combined with lightweight construction techniques (minimal mass and many voids) mean that little heat is either retained within, or conducted into, the building. Low walls and deep eaves reduce the vertical surfaces exposed to solar radiation while reducing glare inside the house. In many cases, grilles and louvred fenestration further fragment the

sunlight entering the building. This results in good illumination, but also disperses the intensity of the sun's rays.

In all these respects the Southeast Asian house presents an admirable solution to the environmental

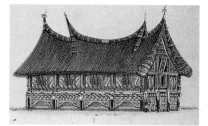

problems posed by living in a hot, humid climate, subject to seasonal monsoon rains. But it should be noted that the house—in the past, as today—is much more than simply a dwelling place, some-where where people eat, sleep and take shelter from the elements. Rather, it is a symbolically ordered structure through which key social

Native Bangalore, Singapore.

values and cultural orientations are expressed. Several of the home owners featured in this book speak of the *karma*, or spiritual qualities, of the houses they live in, and in many Southeast Asian cultures the house is traditionally conceived as a "living" entity, animated by a soul or spirit essence.

Furthermore, the house is often conceptualized in symbolic terms as a mirror image of the universe—a microcosm of the macrocosm. Thus one often finds that the principal house post is represented as a kind of *axis mundi* which centres the house and its occupants in relation to the rest of the universe. Ridge poles, rafters, beams, the hearth and other house parts are also en-dowed with cosmological attributes; they map out the topography of a quasi-mythical universe inhabited by gods, demons, spirits and other supernatural agencies.

TOP RIGHT
The reconstruction of the Royal Palace of Malacca. Such large, two-storey buildings were exclusively built for royalty.

LEFT TOP AND
BELOW RIGHT
Malay houses are always built on stilts *(see drawing by Julian Davison below)*. In the region of Malacca they are distinguished by the addition of a grand staircase of Chinese origin. This stair-case is usually decorated with the same bright tiles imported from Europe that were also used in Chinese shophouses.

FAR LEFT
Today, most well-to-do Malay houses feature a huge four-poster bed draped with colourful quilts. The bed may take on a symbolic importance during wedding ceremonies and other rites of passage.

LEFT
The reception room of this Malay house in Sarawak features Western-style furniture, arranged to receive guests. In more simple homes, most activities take place on the floor, as they do throughout Southeast Asia.

Traditionally, correct orientation in space played an important role in this scheme of things. For example, the east was (and still is) identified with life-giving properties, whilst the west was linked with death—associations which were derived from the rising and setting of the sun. In this respect, the house had to be properly aligned with the sun's path from dawn to dusk so

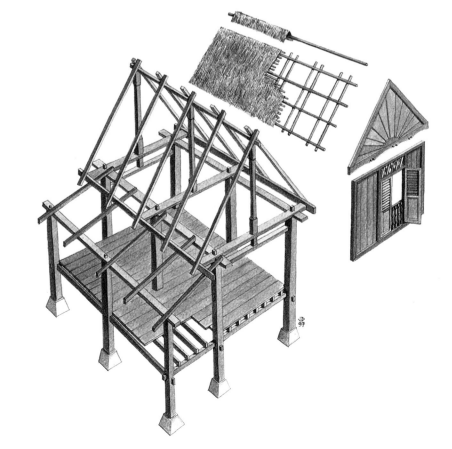

that the rituals of life and death could be performed in the *right* place within the house: one typically finds that women had to give birth in the eastern half of the house, while the dead were laid out in the west. Today, there may be more prosaic explanations for alignment of rooms—whether there is a beautiful view from the verandah for example—but in many cases, present-day owners and architects have consulted ancient traditions in the design of contemporary homes.

In Bali, many expatriates have taken the traditional residential compound as a model for their own homes, adapting local forms to suit their needs. And in Malaysia perhaps the most amenable house form to contemporary lifestyles is the so-called Malacca courtyard house. The Malacca house is already an eclectic mix of Chinese, Portuguese and Malay elements, and the use of brick and tiles as well as timber in the construction, makes it easy to accommodate modern plumbing and sanitation. Fronted by wide verandahs and the floor-to-ceiling fenestration of the typical Malay house, the Malacca version is augmented by a secluded

OPPOSITE TOP
Photograph taken in the 1880s by Charles Kleingrotte or H Stafhell showing two Karo Batak houses to the north of Lake Toba, in Sumatra.

OPPOSITE BOTTOM LEFT
The bamboo roofs and ornamented gable ends of Toraja houses and rice barns, Central Sulawesi. The soaring boat-shaped roof form may be the material legacy of an ancient Austronesian sea-faring past.

OPPOSITE BOTTOM RIGHT
A traditional house from the north of Nias Island, off the west coast of Sumatra, as drawn by the Italian explorer Modgliani in the early years of this century.

TOP
A Javanese *pendopo* at the Sultan's palace, Bangkalang, augmented with European-style Classical columns, circa 1820.

ABOVE LEFT
A *balé*, or open pavilion, typical of an upperclass Balinese residential compound, built for Ida Bagus Tilem, in Mas, Ubud.

LEFT
Illustration by Julian Davison showing joinery details in a Javanese house.

LEFT AND RIGHT
Thai traditional houses are always built on stilts and are composed of several buildings arranged around a central platform.

BELOW
A traditional Laotian house of similar design, depicted here in a chromo-lithograph by the French artist Dela-porte, who accompanied Garnier on his Mekong expedition of 1866.

OPPOSITE TOP LEFT
As the central plains of the Valley of the Chao Praya River in Thailand are extensively flooded for several months each year, many people choose to live on houses floating on bamboo rafts, rather than building on posts which would not rise above the floods. These houses could easily be towed to any convenient location.

OPPOSITE BOTTOM LEFT
Although major Thai temples and Buddhist sanctuaries were built of brick and stone from the very earliest period in Thai history, Thai royalty have preferred, until recently, to live in palaces of wood. This splendid teak wood mansion was once the residence of King Rama I; it was subsequently donated to a monastery (Wat Rakang in Thonburi) for use as the library building. The elaborately carved and gilded door attests to this royal origin.

internal courtyard, sandwiched between other Malay structures. Brick walls, pierced by green-glazed ceramic air-bricks for ventilation, enclose an intimate space, often with a well in one corner. A Chinese-style gateway provides a side entrance and lends a touch of Orientalist whimsy, while potted plants and flowering orchids delight the eye and create a tranquil green space at the very centre of the house.

Traditional Thai architecture is equally amenable to being adapted to modern lifestyles, as first demonstrated by the American, Jim Thompson, in the 1950s *(see pages 14–15)*. Thai houses, like most traditional Southeast Asian timber structures, are put together without any nails or other permanent forms of joinery and can therefore be easily dismantled and reassembled in new combinations to suit the specific demands of the house owner. Like the Balinese pavilion, each building can serve a particular function, providing privacy for guests or quietude for the scholar.
Julian Davison

The Colonial Bungalow

The colonial house in Southeast Asia is the perfect exemplar of Frank Lloyd Wright's famous maxim that beauty—at least of the architectural variety—lies in the relationship of form to function. Simple yet elegant, functional yet comfortable to live in, the colonial house represents a remarkable blend of European and Eastern technologies and sensibilities.

Only the particulars differ from one part of Southeast Asia to another, reflecting the different colonial histories of each region. In this respect, the colonial house is not only a poignant reminder of a bygone era but also a salutary record of the different ways in which the Europeans who came to these eastern countries responded to the colonial encounter.

The Portuguese were the first European power to establish a colonial presence in Southeast Asia in the early 16th century, but little remains from this period by way of domestic architecture. Fortunately, the Spanish, Dutch, English and French have left us with a more substantial architectural legacy in their former colonies: the Spanish in the Philippines, the Dutch in Indonesia, the English in Malaysia and Singapore, and the French in Vietnam, Laos and Cambodia.

In the Philippines, the Spanish initially began by building houses in the manner of their Iberian homeland, but a succession of earthquakes in the 17th century encouraged a greater respect for indigenous building methods. This gave rise to the "stone-wood" house, so called because the ground floor was built of brick and stone, while the upper storey was constructed from wood. The latter was entirely free-standing, being supported on long wooden columns embedded in the ground, and was lightweight and flexible in times of seismic activity. A large overhanging roof afforded protection from the sun and rain.

RIGHT
Early 20th-century "black and white" house in Goodwood Hill, Singapore. While other colonies moved towards a more European type of house in the early years of this century, in the Straits Settlements, the "black and white" bungalow remained the favoured type of dwelling right up until the end of the colonial era.

ABOVE
Photograph taken at the end of the 19th century of a verandah in one of the employee bungalows of the Borneo Company in Chiang Mai. Rattan furniture, polished wooden floors and plaited bamboo walls are all typical features.

LEFT
Louvred fenestration and large open windows invite the outside in, in this example of colonial architecture in Singapore.

Similarly, the Dutch, in Java, began by simply replicating the domestic architecture of their native land—large rectangular houses with symmetrical facades and steeply pitched roofs. In time, however, they incorporated indigenous architectural elements into the design of their houses. This was partly a response to local climatic conditions, but it also revealed a degree of acculturation on the part of the Dutch themselves who were happy to adopt a way of life not too dissimilar to that of the native Javanese. The Dutch Indies' style of domestic architecture reaches its ultimate expression in the great country houses, or *land-huizen*, of the 18th century. These were typically single-storey structures with wide verandahs on all sides, surmounted by a huge hipped roof resembling the *joglo* roof of a Javanese aristocrat's residence.

Sadly, few of these magnificent houses remain, and our knowledge of them comes mainly from written descriptions, old engravings and photographs from the pre-War era.

On the other side of the Malacca Straits, the English also adopted and adapted local architectural traditions in their refinement of the colonial bungalow. This term comes from the Hindi word *bangla*, ("of Bengal") and originally referred specifically to European houses in India. These were generally single-storey residences with a verandah on all sides and a thatched roof with overhanging eaves to keep off the sun's rays. The inspiration for this basic form came, as the name suggests, from native vernacular architecture of Bengal—rude cottages, with curious, crescent-shaped roofs of thatch which were extended in front to create a covered verandah.

In a modified form this basic model was adopted as the archetype for domestic colonial architecture throughout the British Empire.

Early 19th-century bungalows in the Straits Settlements—Penang, Singapore and later Malacca—were thus essentially an Indian import. By this time, however, the original form had undergone substantial modifications and at the upper end of the scale the colonial bungalow was far removed from its humble origins. European influences, and in particular the architecture of Andrea Palladio, had imposed a symmetrical plan and the introduction of an upper storey, or *piano nobile*, as the main living floor. In this last respect, there was an obvious parallel with native Malay houses which were raised on stilts for better ventilation and reduced humidity. Other correspondences

RIGHT
The residence of the British High Commissioner, Eden Hall, has been redecorated in the old colonial style. Rattan furniture, low coffee tables and tall standing lamps would all have been standard furnishings in the last century.

TOP LEFT
A colonial house in Chiang Mai, Thailand, features large overhanging eaves to protect from the sun and rain. A huge rain tree in the foreground provides additional shade.

ABOVE
Painting of the house of the first "White Raja" of Sarawak, James Brooke. Built in the 1840s, it features generous roof eaves to protect from the elements, and a verandah positioned to catch the breezes from the river.

LEFT
A "black and white" house in the Botanic Gardens, Singapore. The flowering palm in the foreground is the Talipot palm, the largest fan palm in the world.

TOP RIGHT
Engraving of an 18th-century Dutch bureaucrat's house in Sulawesi, featuring a mix of European and Eastern traditions in the architecture.

RIGHT
Old postcard of a colonial house in Singapore. The Traveller's Palm (front right), originally from Madagascar, later became synonymous with the island state.

included full-length louvred shutters to maximize the through-flow of air and pitched roofs with overhanging eaves. Furthermore, the verandah was a key element in both architectural traditions. In the case of colonial architecture, the bungalow's essentially rustic nature was ennobled by the use of Classical elements—Etruscan columns and the like—but an overall correspondence between the two architectural types is unmistakable. This was partly due to a kind of parallel evolution—a resort to similar solutions to the problems of designing for the climate—but there also seems to have been a considerable cross-fertilization of ideas between Malay and colonial architectures.

Further to the north, in Indo-China, the French, who were much later arrivals on the colonial scene, were less inclined to respond to local architectural traditions, preferring simply to duplicate the same sort of houses that they lived in back in

France. The old residential districts of Hanoi, Saigon and Phnom Penh, retain to this day an indelible Gaelic stamp, while municipal buildings in

the city centres bask in the arrested afterglow of the Second Empire. A notable exception, is the wonderful French rubber planter's house, near Kuala Selangor in peninsular Malaysia—the famous "Maison des Palmes" which features prominently in Henri Fauconnier's novel of the same name. Although the original structure was destroyed by fire, a new house was built on this site.

This later building consists of a half-sunken basement floor, with masonry walls and stone flags, surmounted by a wooden upper

storey, open on all sides. Wooden internal partitions can be slid back and forth to allow the circulation of air, while spacious verandahs afford a delightful view over the garden.

Perhaps the best-loved example of colonial architecture in Southeast Asia, is the so-called "black and white" architecture of the Straits Settlements. Dating from the

Singapore. European Residence Tanglin.

LEFT
Tilton, a late 19th-century house in Singapore *(see pages 180–181).* Before renovation, this house would have featured open verandahs running round the length of the house.

BOTTOM LEFT
A verandah in a house on Nassim Road, Singapore. Painted black and white blinds or "chicks" can be lowered to protect from sudden rain storms, or to keep out the intense heat of the day.

ABOVE
Built as a house in Singapore in the 1920s, by a wealthy Arab family, the Alkaffs, is now a restaurant.

RIGHT
This 1928 house in Kuching nestles among *nibong* palms. Built in Tudor style, it now houses the Society Atelier Sarawak.

1920s and 1930s, it represents the apotheosis of the colonial style. The ground floor is usually constructed from brick and features a covered porch, or *porte cochère*, constituted by a brace of Etruscan columns on either side of a central arch. The upper storey is of wood—a half-timbered affair, with panels of plastered, plaited bamboo. The main structural elements are typically painted black and the panels white, in the Jacobean manner, giving rise to the label "black and white" as a generic term for this type of architecture. The ground floor usually comprises a spacious reception room and dining area, but the main living space is on the floor above. Here, the rooms are symmetrically arranged, with bedrooms and bathrooms placed on either side of a central salon. The latter extends over the *porte cochère* and is the principal area for socialising: open on three sides, it is the ultimate expression of verandah living. A cantilevered balcony running round the outside of the upper storey connects the bedrooms and bathrooms and provides alternative spaces for domestic activities.

Ultimately, the "black and white" house represents an imaginative and effective response to the problems of tropical design. It selects and combines the most suitable elements from both local and European architectural traditions, and even today, the few remaining examples retain their popularity as expatriate residences.
Julian Davison

"An extension of the internal living space, a verandah creates the ambiguous edge between inside and outside—so typical of well-adjusted dwellings in the tropics."

Robert Powell, architect and author

ON THE VERANDAH

Believed to be Anglo-Indian in origin, the word "verandah" has appeared in a variety of spellings—varanda, viranda, feerandah, to mention only a few. Whichever is used, however, the meaning is clear to anyone who has ever spent time in the tropics—"an open area, usually roofed and sometimes partially enclosed or screened, attached to the exterior of a house or other building."

But this mundane description scarcely does justice to the multi-faceted role played by the verandah in tropical life or to the memories evoked by the word itself. In traditional houses, both local and Western-style, it was perhaps the

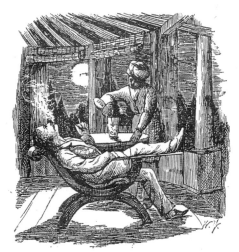

most often-used space, where late afternoon refreshments could be savoured along with views of the garden, where families gathered to catch the evening breezes or watch a monsoon shower, often where meals were taken and business transacted.

"At dawn a boy brought them their tea," Somerset Maugham wrote in one of his Malayan stories, "and they lounged about the verandah, enjoying the fragrance of the morning". In 19th-century Java, a visiting American lady was somewhat taken aback to find all the rooms of her hotel opening on to a common verandah, each section furnished with "lounging-chairs, table, and reading lamp... There is never any jealous hiding behind curtains or screens. The whole hotel register is in evidence, sitting or spread in reclining chairs."

When Colin McPhee rented a house in Bali during the 1930s, he wrote: "the doors creaked; the rooms were musty; the place had been shut a year. But from the deep verandah in front you looked out through the palms over gleaming rice fields and caught a glimpse of the sea beyond."

PREVIOUS PAGE
A verandah in Ubud, Bali:
here the decor is simple to
the point of being spartan
and is reminiscent of the
style favoured by old
plantation bungalows.
However, the view from one
of these rattan chairs looks
out onto an exotic garden,
rather than a lawn and rows
of trees.

OPPOSITE
Old illustration depicting a
colonial scene: an Indian
bearer attends, while the
sahib reclines!

ABOVE
A draped day-bed and
planter's chair, both
upholstered in sumptuous
cool cream, give this
verandah in Legian, Bali,
a feel of the Old World.

LEFT
Designed by the Indonesian
architect, Tan Tik Lam, this
verandah from a modern
house in Bandung, Java, is
perched on the edge of a
dramatic ravine. Continuing
in the tradition of the Dutch
Colonial Art Deco style, the
verandah is extremely tall,
overlooked by both the
ground and upper floors.

ABOVE LEFT
The verandah at the resi-
dence of the British High
Commissioner, Singapore.
Rattan furniture, ceiling fans,
railings and polished wood
floors speak volumes about
the house's colonial past.

ABOVE RIGHT
"Tea on the terrace" in one
of Singapore's "black and
whites". Chicks, or bamboo
blinds painted black and
white, protect the verandah
from direct sunlight, and the
view is of a perfectly
manicured lawn.

RIGHT
A turn-of-the-century
illustration showing four
Dutch officials relaxing on
a verandah in Java.

Modern air-conditioning has elimin-
ated most of the disadvantages
of indoor entertaining, but the
verandah has by no means become
irrelevant or lost its allure. It is still
a significant feature of tropical
architecture, a semi-outdoor living
room where nature becomes part of
the decoration.

Some verandahs are the essence
of simplicity, with polished tiles or
wooden floors worn by bare feet to
a high gloss and little more than a
few comfortable chairs. Others are
more elaborate, with cushioned
furniture, carefully selected artefacts
and masses of potted plants that
bring the garden even closer. Often

there are bamboo blinds that can
be lowered in case of harsh sunlight
or a sudden storm. In either case,
the verandah usually reflects the
character of a house, as much as
does the interior, and it remains an
important centre of its social life.

William Warren

UNASHAMEDLY ROMANTIC
VERANDAH LIVING IN JAVA

GATE OF
CHARITY

GATE OF
FORTITUDE OF MIND

The Jaya Ibrahim House is unashamedly romantic. Sited at the foot of Gunung Salek, a mountain near Bogor in West Java, its cultural pedigree is illusive—it is a hybrid of Javanese, Dutch and, curiously, Venetian influences.

The story of how Jaya, a descendent of the Yogyakarta Royal House of Pakualam, came to design and build the house reads like a romantic novel. In the 1980s while living in London, Jaya narrowly missed acquiring a painting that was auctioned at Christie's: by a 19th-century Dutch artist, it depicted a wedding procession against a backdrop of an imposing mountain (Gunung Salek). The setting entranced him and some time after his return to Java he set out to acquire the site which corresponded to the painting.

Once this transaction was completed, Jaya proceeded to design a building specifically geared towards living in the tropics. The house's narrow plan form permits permanent cross ventilation, while the extensive use of traditional verandahs provides shaded "in-between" spaces which protect and shelter the occupants from the burning sun and violent tropical

OPPOSITE
The house is approached from the west through the "Gate of Bountiful Fortune". The visitor then turns south through an avenue of tropical palms and ascends a broad staircase to the *pendopo* which is on a central axis.

ABOVE
The informal greeting and reception arrangement in the *pendopo*. It is an arrangement not unlike the Malay *serambi*.

LEFT
Looking north from the *pendopo*, a high boundary wall is concealed by a ha-ha, a device borrowed from English landscape designers and often used in stately homes. It permits an uninterrupted view of the surrounding rice fields and connects the house to the land.

"...the extensive use of traditional verandahs provides shaded 'in-between' spaces which protect and shelter..."

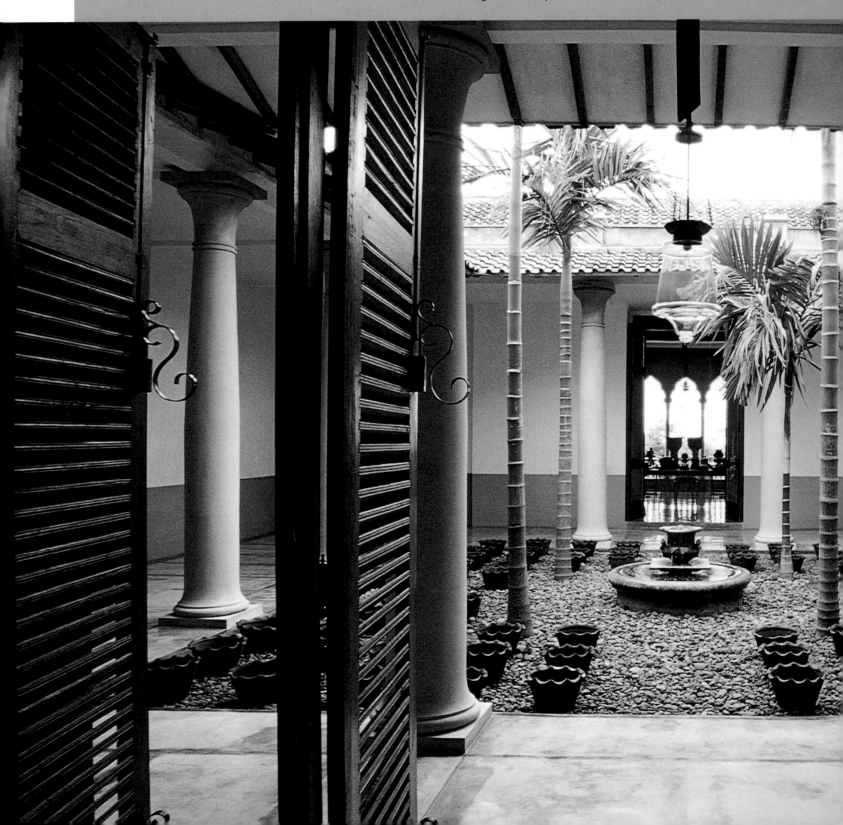

rain storms. Furthermore, they become an extension of the internal living space creating the ambiguous edge between inside and outside which is so typical of well-adjusted dwellings in the tropics.

The house is rather grand. It is entered from the north, on a central axis into a portico, an extended verandah supported on columns. Known in Java as a *pendopo*, it is open on three sides and is used as

BELOW
The east courtyard encircled by a broad verandah which leads to the principal private rooms. Directly ahead is the ante room to the master bedroom.

RIGHT
An informal seating arrangement in the shaded verandah which skirts the east courtyard.

BELOW RIGHT
Mirror and cabinet in one of the bedrooms.

LEFT
One of two principal bedrooms in the east wing. This one opens out to the south-facing verandah and views of Gunung Salek.

BELOW
Looking towards Gunung Salek from the verandah outside the ladies' sitting room. The view of the mountain was the *raison d'être* for the choice of site.

RIGHT
Timber louvred doors open out to the south-facing verandah. Well-constructed houses in the tropics— such as this one—use a minimum amount of glass and are designed for natural ventilation.

an informal reception and greeting area. Directly ahead on the axis is a formal reception and dining room. To the east and west of the central axis are two, almost symmetrical wings, each with a central colonnaded courtyard. The east wing contains the owner's private quarters, while the west wing is principally devoted to kitchens, garages and servants quarters. Along the south-facing facade is a continuous verandah. All the principal rooms open off this verandah or the courtyards, thus ensuring a constant flow of fresh air throughout the house.

Robert Powell

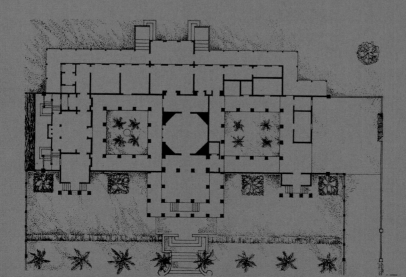

ELEGANT JAPANESE OVERTONES

In many ways, this modern house in Bandung, Java, designed by architect Tan Tjiang Ay, is characterized by its open spaces. These seem to have distinctly Japanese overtones, with pristine lines and a definitive use of running water, wood, bamboo, and other Japanese design elements.

The owner is an art collector, and the walls inside the house are adorned with pieces he has amassed over the years. Outside, however, the decoration is rather more natural. As one enters the compound from the car-park at the front, one is confronted by a walkway with

wooden decking, and a waterfall, complete with running water, river stones and a large collection of ferns. Leading up to the house, the space opens out on to a large covered verandah that fronts an elegant lawn surrounded by trees.

Kim Inglis

LEFT
The long verandah sports wooden beams, wooden decking and is separated from the indoors by extensive, Japanese-style, sliding doors. When these are open, the inside of the house merges with the breeze-cooled exterior. The sound of running water completes the atmosphere.

ABOVE
The view from the verandah is out on to a peaceful lawn.

RIGHT
The covered walkway from the entrance leading up to the house. A cooling effect is achieved the minute one enters the house, by this "avenue" of water, rocks and foliage.

LEFT TOP
To the west stands a high mud wall with thatch covered with orchids. A *lumbung* or rice barn from West Bali has been converted into a playroom.

LEFT MIDDLE
The main living room full of various esoteric objects collected over the years. A teak couch from Madura upholstered in leather stands against the back wall.

LEFT BELOW
The view into the bedroom from the centre of the house. The bed is European style with Chinese motifs. On the back wall is a magnificent *kain inu* ceremonial women's sarong from Lampung, South Sumatra.

BELOW
The main verandah, poised between the garden and the carved splendour of an intricate East Javanese wall.

AN ELABORATE HARLEQUIN PALACE

Author, noted Indonesian art expert and house owner, Bruce Carpenter, describes his verandah lifestyle in Sanur, Bali, thus:

"For centuries, the palaces of Java were made of wood and temples of stone for which reason few truly ancient wooden palaces have survived. The tradition, however, continued in vernacular Javanese houses. In the early 1980s, thousands of these were being demolished, so there were many beautiful architectural elements for sale.

"We decided to buy various pieces and construct a sort of harlequin palace on stilts, as much inspired by Thai and Malay architecture as Indonesian. We found the verandah, where we enjoyed the luxury of being able to live outdoors, the most important part of our home, so we made it almost as large as the actual interior. If you have a great verandah it is obvious that you need a great garden, so we tried to create, as in the interiors, layers of views—hoping to treat the eye not only with the obvious but also with some subtle surprise waiting for discovery."

"The original house on the property, now the Children's House, standing below a very large mango tree, is featured on these two pages. As it was completely closed we built a verandah and kitchen out into the garden. We were determined to avoid a white-washed brick colour scheme, and our inspiration came one day when visiting the home of a Brahmana friend in the village. I noticed that his house had traces of beautiful celadon, apricot and blue pigments, albeit faded and dirty. Excited, I asked him about the colours only to hear that such pastel hues used to be quite common a generation before. Inspired, we decided to experiment with the limited range of paints available. Best of all we were able to break up the white porcelain tiles and replace them with cheap hand-made coloured tiles in green and yellow. The owner of the house thought we were mad!"

TOP LEFT
A pair of 19th-century statues of a royal North Balinese couple in celestial form. Behind hangs a mystical painting from Solo on a carved wood panel.

LEFT
A view from the kitchen out into the garden. The furniture is a mix of new and old: a colonial marble table, rattan chairs and iron chairs which match the celadon floor tiles.

ABOVE MIDDLE
The verandah has marvellous views of the garden. Antique Balinese stone statues line the perimeter.

ABOVE RIGHT
From the corner with the dining table, the verandah wraps around the front of the house where one finds several sitting areas. This antique Javanese couch stands before a Balinese door and looks out into the garden.

RIGHT
A set of teakwood and leather chairs and matching marble table which belongs to the once popular school of Colonial Art Deco and dates from around 1920.

ABOVE
Comfortable rattan sofa and chairs are grouped around a large tea table on the spacious verandah situated beneath the house's stilts.

LEFT
The first-floor verandah opens out onto an ironwood deck; facing the ocean, it offers views of the sunset and capitalizes on breezes coming in from the sea.

BALMY BALINESE AFTERNOONS

A feeling of uncluttered, cool space is achieved by the minimal use of ornamentation on the spacious lower-floor verandah of this beach-front villa in Canggu, in the south of Bali. Sparingly placed Chinese pottery, plants and wooden sculptures contribute to the overall serenity, and allow the surrounding tropical garden to become the main focus of the setting.

The verandah is absolutely huge, as it stretches over almost the whole area of the house. Its size is echoed above it on the first floor, with another verandah which opens out onto a deck. Even though there are other rooms and bedrooms on both these storeys, they are considerably smaller, and the main focus of the house is on these enormous entertaining areas. So, whether it be for an aperitif, a party, a sundown massage or some contemplative meditation, this is the place for it.

Gianni Francione

"The open living room is the heart of the tropical house. Everything else should radiate from it."

Peter Muller, architect

THE OPEN LIVING ROOM

It doesn't take a rocket scientist

to figure out why it feels good to sit in an open living room in a tropical house, but it is surprising how many Westerners are overwhelmed by the idea of a room that invites the world inside. I've even experienced it myself. It's a cold man's logic; as the racially stereotyped Tonto may have noted: pale face from different climate not understand Indian weather.

Interestingly enough, his charge would have been supported by none other than the *Encyclopedia Britannica*. When it comes to domestic construction, it claims that beyond "a single room with sturdy walls and a roof, a door, a window and a hearth...all else is luxury", but I fear the author of this particular section of the pre-digital information bible may have confined his research to the tundra. He missed out, is all I can say.

Consider, for instance, the evolutionary processes involved in this most central of equatorial living quarters—not one part of which should be coloured by Eurocentric bourgeois folly. You live in the tropics (for the purposes of this architectural exercise anyway), where the weather is split predictably into wet and dry seasons. The temperature at your selected site hovers around 30 degrees. The breeze is a welcome visitor and to

be encouraged, while the sun, a hot and often harsh provider, is to be kept at bay (although light, its pale and pleasant relative, is to be shown due hospitality).

All in all, you face a life in a hot and stable climate with a view of a lush river gorge. If you are not lucky enough to have a river gorge (and seasonal variations in wind and rain may dictate a more introspective view, anyway), you face a life in a hot and stable climate with a view of the sky from your living room, probably built as a courtyard or a covered area overlooking a breezy garden. No need for Britannica's walls. A hearth would most certainly be a luxury. Soon enough, you are spending all your time in this indoor-outdoor hybrid, the most natural and harmonious of architectural constructions.

The true experts have long seen reason in this environment-friendly

rationale (let the outside in, it won't hurt you!) yet it is true too that many so-called "modern" Asian cultures fail to find comfort with the open living area, preferring instead the convenience of an air-conditioned apartment bought more as a consanguineous financial investment and less (in my mind at least) as a study of architecture.

"In many ways," the writer Robert Powell noted in his excellent book, *The Asian House*, "the open living room should be the starting point for a tropical house." Or as the Australian architect Peter Muller, famous for the Amandari, Bali, and the Oberois in Bali and Lombok, amongst others, puts it: "The open living room is the heart of the tropical house. Everything else should radiate from it". Everything, that is, except for the fanciful additions of a chicken-hutch mind—like, for instance, the cursed entrance hall. As Muller says: "It always amazes me that people build entrance halls in a tropical house. Why bother? What's the point?"

What is the point indeed? Walls in this context become boundaries; doors and other add-ons a waste

of breeze and light. Glass, an even more superfluous means of confine-ment, is a folly only the foolhardy would consider.

Some might argue that security remains a good enough reason for enclosure, but I wouldn't agree here, either. There are better ways to skin the same cat, as Asian cultures have discovered. A Balinese compound is cradled with-in the safety of a perimeter wall, while the central garden acts as a living area. A Dayak longhouse is lifted above the jungle floor, offer-ing a protected space for life to continue unabated. Both designs offer security from the outside world while allowing other ele-ments—like wind and light—full access to the compound. It's a jug-gling game of climatological and self-preservationary factors that has long been played (and mastered) by traditional Asian cultures. Why mess with it if it works, I have to wonder? As Muller said: "What's the point?"

Why not just sit back and enjoy the view, or is that too much to expect in today's pigeon-hole world?
Nigel Simmonds

PAGES 54–55
Javanese "lattice" windows are the main focal point of this open living room in Legian, Bali. Open to the surrounding tropical garden, they encourage cross-ventila-tion. Cool tiled floors and low, cream-upholstered sofas and planter's chairs create a feeling of space and comfort.

PREVIOUS PAGE
The archetypal tropical living room. Open on three sides, it

features low seating arrange-ments, scatter cushions in "tropical checks" and wooden floors, ideal for bare feet.

RIGHT
An idyllic tropical scene: an open living room is the perfect place in which to hang a hammock and take in the beauty of a scented garden. Lawrence Blair's house in Bali provides just that sensuous opportunity.

PERCHED ON A VOLANIC RIDGE

This house is located high on a ridge to the north of Bandung in West Java. It is surrounded by natural forest, but there are glimpses of the city in the valley below. Tan Tjiang Ay, the architect-owner, lives here for two or three days each week and commutes to work in Jakarta.

Ay has never favoured a sentimental retreat to *alang-alang* and *atap*, but has sought to find a contemporary tropical architectural language which fuses modern materials and functional planning with the wisdom of vernacular architecture. Here, he has found an inspired Modernist solution for a tropical house. He refers to the house plan, somewhat tongue-in-cheek as a "Railway Station type plan". This refers to the simple arrangement where all the main rooms at the first-storey level open onto a linear, glazed living room. Some 15 metres long, this area has sliding glazed windows on three sides, half of which can be opened to allow natural ventilation and an immediate experience of the natural environment. The house is not air-conditioned and the long, narrow plan is ideal for cross-ventilation, permitting a constant relationship with the exterior no matter in which part of the house one is located.

Robert Powell

FAR LEFT
The south-west facing facade of the house permits natural ventilation and a view, through the forest, of Bandung in the valley below.

LEFT AND RIGHT
An extension was built by Tan Tjiang Ay's son (also an architect, Tan Tik Lam) after the main house was completed. Comprising a living room and bedroom, it features double-storey windows that look out over the dramatic view of National Park land *(see right)*.

BELOW
The dining area is an integral part of the linear living space. It has direct contact with the surrounding trees.

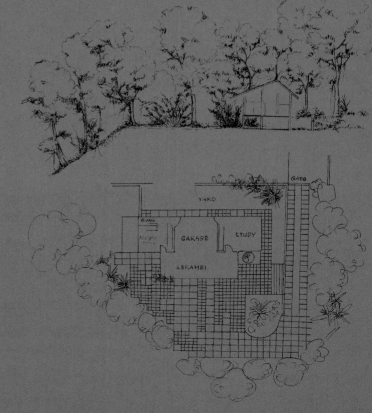

A BREAKFAST ROOM TO DIE FOR...

The Taman Bebek hotel, Madé Wijaya's mountain retreat near Ubud, Bali, is a relatively recent construction. When asked about the concept behind its fabulous open living room, Wijaya says: "This living room overlooks a great view— a horseshoe meander of the mighty Ayung river, the volcanic peak of Mt Batu Karu and a panorama of rice terraces and giant banyan trees. It is essentially a view platform with a '20s colonial theme—a homage to Bali's first European tenant, Colin McPhee, author of *A House in Bali*. The architecture is trad-mod, Balinese with "special effects": the missing corner post, the intrusion of the garden into the sitting area and the nod to Japanese architecture in the detailing of the bedroom above.

"The giant octagonal coconut wood posts are idiosyncrasies that make this house unique. Copied from Peter Muller's reworking of Rudolf Bonnet's original studio in Campuan, they sit on large flat river boulders. The decor is a hodge-podge of Dutch, Australian and Portuguese colonial. Indonesian folk elements, such as the colourful carved doors and Javanese statuary, add an eclectic "Ubud" feel. Of particular note is the rare shell-inlaid door from Nusa Penida off the coast of Bali."

OPPOSITE
Three-seater sofa, salvaged from the builder Pak Dapat's house: a '70s classic, it was modelled on an 18th-century Portuguese chair once found in Puri Gianyar palace.

LEFT
The view across the valley. On occasions, on full moon nights, Wijaya puts hundreds of candles on the banks of the river below. The cosy confines of the room and the dark brick flow lend a "signal box" atmosphere to the setting.

BELOW
Wicker chairs designed by Nevile Marsh for the Hotel Saba and an Australian bush table anchor the room's "view-perch" corner.

A PAINTED HOUSE

I designed the Presidential Suite in the Taman Bebek as a successor to the cozy cottage *(see page 92)* that had served me, more than admirably, for over ten years. I wanted a house for the Ubud of the '90s, something larger, with more modern entertainment areas and a bit of glamour to keep up in the designer's showpiece stakes!

Australian painter Stephen Little advised on all the finishes: the result is a testament to the power of the decorative arts over slightly stolid architecture! Large bamboo furniture by Putu Suarsa of Big Bamboo and a dizzying array of pan-Pacific kitsch—matador lamps, a table painted with figures of Tin-Tin by Australian painter Jason Blakelock and the spice island neo-Adam shell chandelier—all add a needed touch of whimsy to what threatened to be an "Amanwanabe"!

Madé Wijaya

BELOW
Painting by Andrew Logan of the garden and bedroom wall as seen from the open living room *(on right)*.

ABOVE
Door with painted star motif leading to the living room.

RIGHT
The entrance vestibule "breeze-way" features a 1930s mirror from a gold dealer's shop in Bukittinggi, West Sumatra, and some inspired *trompe l'oeil* drapery by artist Stephen Little.

TOP MIDDLE
On the bar counter, a dutch potty with pink *ti* plants is framed by painted shutter doors. Inspired by Toraja cloth patterns; the shutters seal off the bar/office.

TOP RIGHT
The main living room and party terrace. The giant limestone table is by artist Shane Sweeney. The backdrop to the living room is the dawn-hued wall to the Royal Suite Cottage *(see pages 96–97)*. The giant terracotta pot in the garden is an indigo vat used for making batik in Java in the 19th century.

LEFT
Painting by Stephen Little of a corner of the living room, alongside a path and Balinese gate. It illustrates perfectly how a well-designed open living room truly blends in with the surrounding garden in a tropical setting.

BELOW
The pool and adjacent massage, siesta and cocktail pavilion are the "focus and folie" of the compound.

A BEACH HOUSE IN BALI

This compound in Canggu, a rural village near Kuta, was designed for a group of Jakarta-based executives. They wanted a retreat, near the ocean beaches of Kuta-Legian-Canggu, but with a Balinese country feel. The virgin site sloped down to a shapely meander in the Canggu River, with stunning views west to the rice fields and a beautiful temple. As it was to be a holiday house for the beach fun set

I kept it fairly open to catch the sea breezes and extraordinary afternoon light.

The pool and pavilion are the focus and heart of the compound. The five bungalows and two entertainment areas are positioned on interlocking terraces which define a structured Balinese palace feel. The style of the interiors is "rustic-charm" with a nod to the colonial

Denpasar look with which I had experimented, with success, at the Villa Bebek and the Hotel Saba. Jakarta friend, Ruby Illi, worked with us on the interiors, adding a dash of Jakarta trendiness.

The full-on Balinese tropical garden with classical artwork accents blends in with the verdant temple valley in which the compound nestles.

Madé Wijaya

BELOW
The sitting room in the main house: the Balinese baronial theme of the interiors suits the soaring ceilings and masculine architectural lines.

OPPOSITE TOP LEFT
The curve of the steps mirrors that of the pool.

OPPOSITE TOP RIGHT
Watercolour by Stephen Little showing the view of the Balinese temple nestling in the valley below.

A JAVANESE DREAM HOUSE

BELOW AND OPPOSITE
BOTTOM
The double-doored entrance
to the house, accessible
from the ground by wooden
steps, leads into the "hold-
ing pen", the reception/
dining area prior to the
main room *(see overleaf)*.

Aided by two Javanese master craftsmen, my brother Lorne spent about six years meticulously assembling this three-storey, three-bedroom, two living-room home, from 100-year-old carved teak salvaged from old East Javanese rice granaries. The whole affair is raised four feet above the ground on stilts (a surprising rarity in Bali, although common elsewhere in Indonesia), to provide an additional storage area, ventilation and protection from ground damp.

The kindness of the wood on bare feet and the vulnerability of the house to aromatic breezes and passing butterflies, makes for a very sensuous living experience. Bamboo blinds protect the house from all but the horizontal rain which occurs every seven years or so with a violent southern wind which the locals call the "building inspector".

Lawrence Blair

ABOVE
Wooden railings separate
the living area from the
garden.

RIGHT
The exterior of the house:
Unusually for a Balinese
house, the whole construction is raised four feet
above the ground on stilts.
This elevates the structure
and encourages cross-
ventilation.

OPPOSITE
The stairway between the reception and the main living rooms ascends past early Javanese panelling up to the three progressively more organic storeys of the house.

LEFT
The large *balé*, or traditional Balinese sprawling place, in the main living room, with the final level, housing a library, perched above it.

BELOW
The top bedroom, at coconut height, with sliding glass windows on three of its five sides, looks over miles of rice paddies down to the sea.

BOTTOM
The main, and more private of the two living rooms: a surface of seasoned teak "floating" above the vegetation, as viewed from the introvert's end of the room.

A HYBRID HOLIDAY BUNGALOW

A rooftop aerie, a large living room open on two sides, Javanese motifs on the lintels and abundant use of wood and white are only some of the unusual features in this seemingly straightforward house. Situated in Legian, Bali, it is at first glance simple in construction and layout; only when one looks at the details does it become apparent that such glances can be deceptive.

The elegantly simple living space, 'which is separated from the garden by a large column and further wooden posts, exploits the çandour of white upholstered furniture, a white tiled floor and a central white-washed concrete structure. As a contrast, warm hues are created by the bamboo-thatched roof, the beams on the ceiling and the colonial antique furniture. Comfortable cushions, a local rug and various Southeast Asian artefacts complete the scene. Similarly, the vibrant tones of the surrounding tropical garden add a splash of colour.

Gianni Francione

FAR LEFT
A night-time view of the house, clearly showing the snug bedroom with accompanying verandah at the top, and the open living room below.

CENTRE
Javanese day beds and wicker planters' chairs—and a colourful tropical garden—create a contemporary colonial-style interior.

ABOVE
The use of wood and white—and a few assorted ornaments—contribute to the overall simple but effective feel of the interior.

LEFT
One of the understated design elements in this house is the use of geometric Javanese motifs set in plaster above the doors. Built-in sofas and whitewashed walls keep the area cool and clean. A wooden staircase leads up to the loft bedroom.

ABOVE
The living area on the upper
floor commands uninterrupted
views over rice fields.

OPPOSITE TOP
The roof lines interplay with
the different levels between
the dining and living areas.

OPPOSITE BOTTOM
The geometric complexity of
the roof is shown here on
the exterior *(see drawing)*,
and inside *(see photograph)*.
The designers use local
materials and reinterpret
them in a Modernist style.

RIGHT
An atmospheric view of the
house at sunset.

A DEFINING ROOF

Located in a residential area on the south coast of Bali, this villa is a synthesis of elements typical of local architecture and those of a modern European character. Designed by Gianni Francione and Mauro Garavoglia of Studio Hutter Associates, the house is set on three different levels, each following the natural slope of the site. Each storey gives direct access to the garden and a different view of the surrounding area.

The main entrance leads into a balconied living space which overlooks a lower mezzanine dining area—both creating an open social space. The bedrooms are on the lowest level, and remain separate. The defining roof is the fundamental architectural element. Always visible from the inside, its articulate form defines the contours and layout of the spaces below. The very low pitches create a sensation of intimacy and security.

Gianni Francione

LEFT TOP
A view of the villa's spectacular swimming pool.

LEFT BOTTOM
The roof of the living area is clad internally with woven matting and externally with Borneo wood shingles. The furnishing has been kept to a minimum, in order to allow views of the garden to predominate.

CONTINUITY OF SPACE

ABOVE
The living area is totally open to the garden. Here, a view of the stairs leading up to the second floor. The floor is made from *bengk-erai* wood, and the walls are clad with local ivory-coloured and grey stone called *paras.* The combination of the two creates a subtle patterning effect.

Another house by Gianni Francione and Mauro Garavoglia of Studio Hutter Associates, this large two-storey holiday villa in Kerobokan, Bali, fuses elements of Western architectural culture with the splendid building traditions of Bali.

The stark geometry of the roof defines the principal lines of the internal spaces. The ridge of the main roof corresponds to a walkway which connects the spaces on the first floor. To accentuate this continuity of space, the upper balconied level overlooks the

entertainment area below. This is divided into an open sitting area with a dining part behind. It is illuminated by artificial lighting, which utilizes the roof as a reflecting surface, and casts a soft, mellow hue around the interior.

There is an abundant use of natural materials in the finishes: *bengkerai* wood on the floor, *paras* cladding on the walls, woven matting on the roof and wood shingles from Borneo on the roof's exterior, are vernacular touches.

A fantastic entertainment area that is totally open to the surrounding garden completes the house design. Comprising a lily-moated square pavilion, connected to the main house by a covered walkway, this simple detached structure was inspired by the the traditional Balinese *balé* design. Here, however, it takes on a new form. Managing at once to both break up and balance the volume of the main corps of the house, it becomes the focal point of the whole structure and an ideal spot for both dining and relaxing. All the while, it offers amazing views over the garden and swimming pool, and to the rice-terraced valley beyond.

Gianni Francione

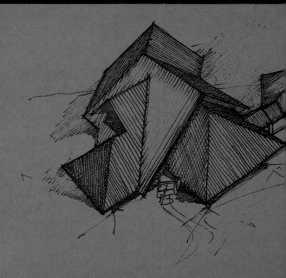

OPPOSITE TOP
The external walkway connecting the living zone to the detached dining pavilion stretches above a carpet of pebbles.

OPPOSITE BOTTOM
View of the all-open dining pavilion. The very low pitches of the roof maximize the intimate feel of the tiny. Built-in sofas offer a relaxing seating area to take in the amazing views.

ABOVE
View of the dining pavilion from across the lily pond.

LEFT
View of the same house showing the dining pavilion *(at right right)*. The whole structure is a remarkable example of Western modern organic design ideas inspired by vernacular architectural elements.

LEFT
A portable computer on a
splendid antique Javanese
bureau: this combination
of the traditional and the
contemporary reflects the
spirit of the house.

RIGHT
Detail of the overhanging
eaves at the entrance of the
house.

BELOW
An angle of the living area
open to the external jungle
features an antique Javanese
tea-table and an array of
traditional ethnic objects.

BELOW RIGHT
View of the living room
looking in: a separate open
dining space is visible on
the right.

OVERLEAF
Exterior of the villa: set in
a lush tropical garden, the
villa combines vernacular
style with a modern twist.

A CONTEMPORARY VISION OF SPACE

Designed by Gianni Francione, this house in south Bali reproposes traditional Balinese architecture with a contemporary vision of space. A constant interplay of varying levels and volumes creates a succession of spaces, passages and apertures.

The extensive use of *bengkerai* wood is duly balanced by low walls in *paras*—a soft local stone—and ivory-washed surfaces. The effect is a soft luminous quality totally open to and in harmony with the luxuriant nature of the surrounding garden; here palms, mangoes and fragrant frangipani trees flourish within a canvas of close-clipped lawns.

The furnishings also reflect the owner's passion for Indonesian tribal art: textiles, sculptures, plates, bowls, rattan woven baskets from Borneo, antique mats and other carefully selected items, testify to the extraordinary heritage of the various Indonesian peoples and their art.

Gianni Francione

UNDER THE MOSQUITO NET

"Dream platforms—the allure

of the net-draped bed;

everyone should experience

a tropical night at least once."

Madé Wijaya, designer

PREVIOUS PAGE
This dream colonial-style bedroom at the palatial Begawan Giri villas near Ubud, Bali, is an excellent example of landscape as interior design. The bedroom leads into a secluded bathroom courtyard, while the bed is captured under a canopy and the dramatic form of a thatch roof.

LEFT
This compound in Ubud, Bali, often acts as home to visiting pop stars and the international glitterati. Here, a single room—perched on the edge of a deep ravine with fabulous views—comprises a bedroom cum study in one.

The nocturnal symphony of the tropics—the frogs, cicadas and gamelan sounds—are all the more entrancing when experienced from within the cozy confines of a net-draped four-poster bed.

Ideally, this should be situated on a wide verandah or in a room open on at least one side (preferably to a Rousseau-esque garden). Secluded, yet open, the area within such a bedroom in a tropical house then becomes the heart and hearth of muggy climes.

The raised platform bed—often piled high with embroidered throw cushions, and that staple of sweaty sleep, the sausage-like bolster known as the "Dutch wife"—is an instant ticket to siesta satisfaction.

Be it a Chinese opium bed, an iron colonial or a *taban* platform in a Balinese pavilion, the feeling of climbing up into a gossamer cage is as tropical as the mosquito coil and the bamboo blind.

It is my view that one has not experienced the tropics without having spent a wet season night, alive with its waves of water crashing around the eaves, from within the confines of such a gossamer cage dream platform.

Madé Wijaya

SLEEPING UNDER THE STARS

I designed a series of trad-mod houses for this complex in the years from 1980 to 1992. The last was a villa for Helen and Rolf Von Büren where the entire upper floor is an open bedroom *(on right)*. It has a lavishly carved and painted four-poster bed by old Bali-hand Max Weber. The house sits on an estuary on a beach lagoon—with the bedrooms surveying splendid views of the Indian Ocean and the volcanic peaks on the isle of Java beyond. The sunsets are quite simply sensational.

On the practical side, the sleeping platform is secured from swamp monsters by a mosquito net which folds down from the pavilion's eaves. The bathroom is on the garden level below: fine views of rice paddies can be experienced from a special bathing pavilion. Set into the ceiling of the pavilion *(above left)* is a carved ridge plate from an old Balinese ceremonial pavilion. The double volume loggia connects the bedroom with the garden which is often used for parties and dance performances.

Famed on the island—and further afield—the Von Büren's compound is noted for the high-Bali style of its entertainments.

Madé Wijaya

ABOVE LEFT
Star motif set on a carved ridge plate above the bed.

ABOVE RIGHT
Painting by Stephen Little showing the entrance to the Von Büren house.

OPPOSITE TOP
Stephen Little watercolour showing the view out to the sea—and a plan of the house illustrating its relation to the lagoon it is situated around, and the Indian Ocean.

RIGHT
The romance of "sleeping under the stars": the bedroom is open on all sides, and affords fabulous views over the Indian Ocean, and to Java beyond.

OPEN-AIR DREAM PLATFORMS...

Both of these bedrooms were originally living rooms in totally open-sided pavilions. They were later converted by Madé Wijaya with the addition of internal tent-like structures.

At tropical dawn, a symphonic overture of bird sounds, accompanied by a crescendo of golden light, acts as a soul-warming *reveille*. On moonlit nights the palm leaves cast shadows against the pattern of the netting and one experiences the "moon-baking" that brings on that delightful state known as "going troppo"! Such rooms, while ideal for honeymooners, are no good for night owls.

The bedroom *(on left)* is situated in the Taman Bebek hotel with views over the Ayung River gorge. The floor and main pavilion structure are made from coconut wood. The Bridal Suite in the Villa Bebek compound *(on right)* receives cooling breezes from all sides and has views from above over the surrounding garden and lily pond.
Madé Wijaya

TOP LEFT
At the Villa Bebek, Sanur, Bali, a jug with flowers against a backdrop of carved wood.

TOP RIGHT
Light and shadow play an important role at the Villa Bebek. Stone carvings add a textured feel, while colour is used creatively.

ABOVE
A bedroom in the Taman Bebek hotel near Ubud, Bali. The bed is a primitive piece from Madura: it has two 1930s Buicks carved and painted on its headboard!

LEFT
Drawing of a Balinese gate at the Villa Bebek, by Peter Wright.

BELOW
The Bridal Suite at the Villa Bebek. A rich mix of artifacts from Lombok, Bali, Madura, Java and Morocco create an Aladdin's cave of colour and artistry. The snake painting is by Ian Van Wieringin. The bedside lamps were designed by Madé Wijaya.

A "DIAMOND VILLA" IN THE TROPICS

The owner of this open, spacious home located in a former Sanur palm grove named his house "Villa Intan" in deference to the many *intan*, or diamond, motifs that were inadvertently created by an extensive use of wood lattice in the home's original construction. This motif is not just a functional wall detail but also—in enlarged forms—a design theme below second-floor railings and between first-floor window frames. The generous use of criss-crossing wood achieves both a sense of grand openness and an inexpensive form of natural air-conditioning.

Indeed, on the structure's second floor one literally lives in constant harmony with the balmy out-of-doors, separated from nature only (when one wishes) by large hand-loomed curtains that can be drawn across the length of the house as

they would be across a stage. Also available are locally-made bamboo screens or *crey* that can be rolled up or down as necessary. Living spaces up there, including a large bath and wardrobe area, are "separated" only by mobile, traditional Javanese barrier screens which allow for constant interior design changes. Every corner of this upstairs aerie offers panoramic views of a rambling tropical garden and four other Bali-style homes. Yes, birds, butterflies and even bats can fly in and out of here as they wish.

The overall effect is a huge second floor "loft" space that serves triple purposes as a writing and graphic design studio, bedroom and enter-taining area. An all-purpose and eminently troppo salon, as it were, that can quickly become private or public depending on the day's mood.

Leonard Lueras

OPPOSITE TOP FAR LEFT
A large central greensward and waving coconut palms provide a cool garden setting for the Villa Intan.

OPPOSITE TOP MIDDLE
This carved Balinese face is a second-floor support post detail.

OPPOSITE TOP RIGHT
During the day, old lace mosquito nets or *kelambu*, are fastened up with silver hooks wrought and engraved in the form of diamond-eyed tropical birds. The bed is an antique four-poster called a Raffles Bed.

OPPOSITE BELOW
A minimal use of furniture and Afghan *kilim* rugs, plus the luxury of a splendidly high bamboo and thatch roofline make for great spaciousness in Villa Intan's second-floor loft area. Antique brass lamps from a Javanese palace illuminate this rambling room.

ABOVE
This upstairs sitting nook, with a marble-topped table from Singapore and a hand-carved day bed from the East Java island of Madura, can be utilized for work or leisure.

LEFT
This bed belonged to a theatrical impresario in Central Java—it's certainly camp enough! The painting behind it is by Stephen Little. At the foot of the bed is a gold stencilled box sourced by antiquary Wieneke de Groot of Jakarta. Woven bamboo screens are pressed between light crimson rafters on the ceiling.

RIGHT
The doors to the bathroom are copies of life-size 18th-century Javanese glass paintings of nobles attired in court dress.

THE ROYAL OPULENCE OF TAMAN BEBEK

With a view to die for, and a verandah along one side, the Royal Suite in the Taman Bebek hotel, must be the *crème-de-la-crème* of tropical bedrooms. Designed by Madé Wijaya in 1993, it combines the open air, soft furnishings, opulence, and an almost impossibly romantic atmosphere....

Wijaya describes the process that led to his designing it: "As I grew up in Bali, I realized I needed a room for ambassadors and pop stars (either that or I would be relegated to the by-lines' section of the glossies! Ha!)." Thus was born the Royal Suite, realized by Australian artist Stephen Little.

"I put all the best pieces I had from 20 years antique hunting at Stephen's disposal—and let him loose with a dud cheque and his wild imagination. He knows I love the 'Umbria-grunge' look and

'50s follies: I think the resultant decorative finish is a gem. The modernist louvred 'Queenslander' doors lead onto a terrace overlooking the verdant excesses of the Ayung River valley. The room never fails to impress the glamour-weary—its combination of Old World charm and drop-dead view recalls the *folie* bedrooms in the villas that dot Sintra, Portugal's 'Ubud', which acted as the room's inspiration."

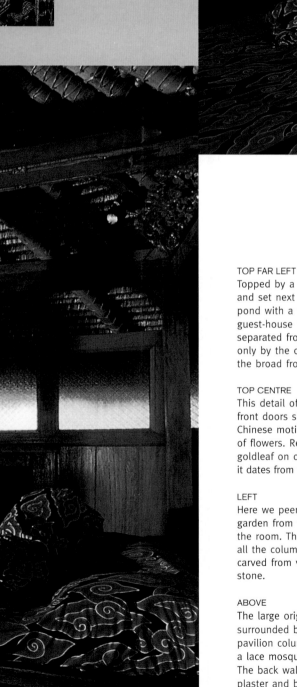

A CELESTIAL GUEST HOUSE

TOP FAR LEFT
Topped by a thatched roof and set next to a small koi pond with a waterfall, the guest-house bedroom is separated from the garden only by the open carving of the broad front doors.

TOP CENTRE
This detail of the folding front doors shows a classical Chinese motif with a vase of flowers. Rendered in goldleaf on cinnabar paint, it dates from the 19th century.

LEFT
Here we peer out into the garden from the inside of the room. The bases of all the columns are hand-carved from volcanic tuff stone.

ABOVE
The large original bed is surrounded by four of the pavilion columns from which a lace mosquito net is hung. The back wall is from plaster and brick with a Balinese door leading to the bathroom.

For years we were guests of others, so when it was time to build our own guest house we really wanted something both simple and elegant. It all began when I bought an early 19th-century traditional pavilion or *balé gede*. This in fact consisted of little more than 12 carved columns and various cross beams with traces of cinnabar and goldleaf over exquisite carvings.

As Sanur can be quite hot and muggy, we decided to build on stilts, both for aesthetic effect and for cross-ventilation. The floor and walls are of wood all on the same level. We were able to remove one of the beds to create a fairly large space for a table and armoire. While they look original to the building the front doors are actually from China and were ordered by a wealthy overseas Chinese merchant in the Riau archipelago.

Bruce Carpenter

BALI NATURAL
MEETS WESTERN
OPULENCE

It's not surprising there are similarities between Madurese designer, Amir Rabik's home close to Ubud in Bali and those of several other lotus-consuming residents of the sunny isle. If he hasn't designed them himself, his influence on the jungle-tropical style is echoed in many of the island's houses. The universal references are there to see—*alang-alang* roofs and bamboo/coconut wood structures; a cornucopia of Indonesian and Dutch colonial furniture; rooms open to the view, and bedrooms where sleep—one suspects—must come as smoothly as the passage of the sun over Bali's extravagant horizon. Rabik's home, a pioneer of the hybrid, heady mix of Bali-natural-meets-Western-opulence style, mixes a narcotic stew of vernacular architecture with personal design follies, including a studio where mirrored panes are interspersed with regular glass, creating a bizarre reflective wall that echoes the strange and magical ambience of a shadow-dappled site.

Nigel Simmonds

OPPOSITE TOP
The exterior of Amir Rabik's extraordinary pavilion-style house near Ubud, Bali.

OPPOSITE MIDDLE
The bedroom on the ground floor doubles up as a living area open to the elements outside. Coconut pillars support a bamboo and thatch roof in the ground-floor space, where edges are blurred between sleeping and living quarters.

ABOVE
The bedroom on the first floor of Rabik's Ubud home leverages a magnificent view over the sacred Ayung River valley.

RIGHT
Steps, inlaid with river pebbles, lead up to the raised ground floor.

LEFT
The double-draped inner space encasing the bed is private and precious—it creates what must be one of the most romantic bedrooms in Bali! Situated in Legian, one cannot fail to fall in love with (or in) this house's bedroom.

BILLOWING MAGIC

A raised central platform, a simple draped wooden structure, a pure white mosquito net cascading from the centre of the roof: the components of this magnificent bedroom are basic, but their skillful combination creates an extremely impressive result.

The four posters and the beams delimiting the sleeping area are made of soberly carved teak. In the centre a white balustrade forms the headboard for a Javanese-style bed that rests on mats from Borneo.

White-washed walls and a traditional roof of bamboo *alang-alang* pleasantly offset the built-in mirrored wardrobe *(in background)*. The floor is polished ivory terrazzo with square black inserts, softened with antique rugs from Borneo and Chinese pottery. On either side, beneath carved wooden appliqués (antique Madurese *gerobohs*), two pairs of old, traditional Javanese sculptures stand as sentinels over this magical dreamtime space.

Gianni Francione

LEFT
Built-in bed in the rear of the house is framed in wooden "lace". These carved eave brackets probably supported temple or palace roofs in the past. Because the house is open on three sides, sleep is peaceful due to the cross-ventilation of sea breezes.

RIGHT
The wide verandah facing the sea is the main meeting place in the house.

BELOW
The main room of the house is simple and compact. A clearing in the palm-plaited roof creates a space for a sleeping loft accessible by ladder. Lacquered folding screens from Burma separate the living area.

BOTTOM
Sunset from the verandah.

OVERLEAF
In another of the three houses that make up this residence, this bed in the loft is a truly romantic nest.

BENEATH KRABI'S LIMESTONE CLIFFS

Railay Beach, near Krabi in southern Thailand, may not be everyone's idea of a tropical paradise, but to a small group of people who built 17 houses there in 1985, it comes close to it. Limited electricity, no hot water, outside bathrooms, no easy access and no air-conditioning are simply small inconveniences to the residents of Lanka Daeng. Set against a backdrop of 100-metre-high limestone karst cliffs, these traditional Thai-style houses are all constructed of prefabricated teak and raised above the ground. Embellished with carved fretwork, they have steep roofs with wide overhanging eaves providing shade. At their bases, there are small water fountains to wash sandy feet.

In this property, comprising three separate structures, the margins between inside and outside are blurred as large shuttered windows and doors open onto verandahs connected by tribal rugs. Closeted beneath a mosquito net in any of the beds, one has fabulous views out over the sea. And sound sleep is guaranteed, as—caressed by sea breezes—one drops off to the sound of the waves lapping on the shore.

Over the years, the owner has amassed a collection of textiles and lacquerware from Southeast Asia. These, along with the cushions and rugs scattered throughout, produce an ethnic aesthetic entirely in keeping with the architectural style.
Kim Inglis

"Oh, for the great outdoors—bogs in the bush or garden bathrooms, in Bali and beyond..."

Madé Wijaya, designer

THE OPEN BATHROOM

In 1972, architect Peter Muller's garden bathroom for the Kayu Aya Hotel (now the Oberoi) in Legian, Bali, created a real sensation. His work in Australia in the 1950s and 1960s showed a deep respect for Japanese architecture and a love of timber-framed structures, but it was not until he "discovered" Bali in 1969 that his most enduring legacy was born.

This was a seminal bathroom design that has now been cloned in every dream home or villa hotel from Honolulu to Hanoi.

Muller is a "pavilion style" architect with a design philosophy based on respect for nature and natural materials. He designs tropical buildings in the tradition of the great colonial architects, like Lutyens and Bawa, but also in the spirit of the ancient palaces of Bali, Java, China, India and Japan. In his architecture, or environmental design, the courts are as important as the buildings which enclose them—hence the outdoor element in the bathroom. Among his gifts to the tropical design world are the Amandari pool, the limestone rubble wall, the idea of interlocking

PREVIOUS PAGE
Huge lotus-shaped bathtub in a house in Ubud, Bali: the view from here is over a stunning ravine.

OPPOSITE BOTTOM
Peter Muller's original bathroom design at the Oberoi in Legian, Bali. Muller set the standard: the bathrooms were open to the sky and the garden beyond.

LEFT
Custom-built terrazzo vanity counters are all the craze in Bali's beachside suburbs. The niche garden provides light and ventilation.

BELOW
This Balinese version of the Hawaiian garden jacuzzi is styled in a classical Roman bath manner. Balinese soap-stone masonry and a sunken terrazzo tub contrast with the lush mossy courtyard.

courtyards and pavilion scapes as viable alternatives to high-rise hotel housing, and of course his fabulous outside-inside bathroom design. Inspired by Balinese *mandi* bathing springs and the indoor-outdoor bath-houses of the traditional Balinese house, his design introduced carefree *joie-de-vivre* to an area that had previously been strictly closeted.

The next two decades saw the garden bathroom craze grow to startling proportions in Bali: it was not until Nancy Kissinger discovered a snake in her bath tub that glass doors were introduced in many houses! But garden bathrooms they remained, with a healthy emphasis on tropical garden enjoyment during ablutions.

Outdoor showers in garden bathrooms have now become fashionable in all the six-star villa hotels and the island's dream homes. And the design theme has spread all over the tropical world—and beyond. I fancy that the new trend for hotel bathrooms with a view had its beginnings in the magical *mandis* of the fabled isle!

Madé Wijaya

BELOW
This niche leads to a sun-filled garden courtyard complete with statue. The soft eggshell grey wall finish and *dado islamique* are by Stephen Little.

OPPOSITE TOP LEFT
Bathrooms at the Taman Bebek hotel have a wardrobe/vanity section which is glassed in, then an outdoor ablutions section in a walled garden court; this is a practical combination, for reasons of humidity and security.

OPPOSITE TOP RIGHT
This rather grand bathroom door leads down to a spacious garden bathroom in the original Von Büren house at "Seaview", Brawa *(see pages 90–91)*. Only "pure" Balinese pavilions were used for most of the complex.

OPPOSITE BELOW
The garden bathrooms of Puri Canggu Mertha feature apricot blush terrazzo tubs. These were invented by Ed Tuttle for Adrian Zecha during the desecration of Donald Friend's famed compound at Batu Jimbar in Sanur, and later championed by Linda Garland in her upgrade of Geoffrey Bawa's House "A" for Vivian Assa.

FOUR BREEZY BATHROOMS IN BALI

Designer Madé Wijaya describes four open bathrooms he has designed in Bali:

"These bathrooms were done for clients who love traditional Balinese architecture and aren't overly fussy about privacy. Gardens reflected in mirrors, towels hanging on wooden pegs in the sun and the bathing space in a drying breezeway are elements I hold dear when designing a bathroom space.
I like the feel of timber floors under foot with generous rugs to sop up excess moisture and cream West Javan marble, which matches the limestone trim, the bamboo, coconut wood and thatch in the architecture. The garden then provides the contrast."

LEFT TOP
The pair of barber-pole lights in this elegant niche echo the Venetian folie theme in the master suite of Ibrahim's "Hacienda Javanica" outside Bogor, West Java.

LEFT BOTTOM
Javanese *Wayang* paintings, a 19th-century noble-woman's beauty case and other assorted palladia refine this sitting room.

BELOW
Gunung Salek, the holiest mountain of pre-Islamic West Java, as viewed from a sunning terrace off Ibrahim's spacious guest bathroom.

JAVA'S ANSWER TO PALLADIO

Jaya Ibrahim is Java's answer to Palladio, with a healthy dash of Belgravia. His bathroom designs for his two Jakarta houses exhibit the severe but simple lines of the cavernous Dutch bathrooms of the colonial era with their high ceilings and generous shower cubicles. His Calvinism-conscious concrete finishes remind one of the remedial virtues of rough soap and cold water—a quirkish nod to boarding-room basic.

To soften this image, Ibrahim adds his collector's touch of rare prints and *objets trouvées*. "*Losmen* chic" was the label one American art critic attached to them.

In his house in Bogor *(see pages 40–45)*, the bathrooms *(featured here)*, seem somehow softer in style. And, of course, the open air is added for refreshing measure.
Madé Wijaya

OPPOSITE
Light streams through the skylight in this hexagonal bathroom creating a magical play of water, shadow and foliage.

RIGHT
With a skylight above, the bathroom is alive with stone reliefs in the wall and a celestial nymph from whose hands the shower's waters tumble.

BELOW
On either side of the sink one finds an array of objects, vases, candles, Javanese angels and an inlaid terracotta relief. This can be re-arranged to fit the mood.

A MEDITATIONAL BATH

"So much of our life is spent in bathrooms that one could even argue that they are the most important rooms in a house," says Bruce Carpenter. "The Balinese associate their spring-fed bathing places with the meditation caves of the ascetics who once used them. Bathing is not only about cleaning the body but also the mind. That is why my wife and I sought to create a space that has the feeling of a meditation cave with subdued light, rich earth colours and wonderful works of art to please the mind and body—just like the caves of one thousand Buddhas."

A WATERPLAY GARDEN

The hexagonal bathroom at Lorne Blair's house in Bali (see pages 70–73) is described by his brother, Lawrence, thus:

"The roof, which partially covers the bathroom, catches and channels fresh water, while its struts are of antique teak tiled with ironwood shingles. Paved with celadon slate, and partially walled with thin volcanic *paras*, it is less a bathroom than a water-play garden, which is particularly inviting under the light of a full moon or in the firefly season."

SMALL SPACES IN THE BIG CITY

As the concept of the open bathroom began to gain popularity, contemporary architects started to experiment with ways in which the design could be used in renovated or modern houses in urban settings.

Space, of course, was the main consideration: in hotel complexes or in country houses, private gardens with outside views are not difficult commodities. In the city, it is an entirely different matter. Architects have risen to the challenges posed by space constrictions, by employing natural materials in the small spaces available—pebbles, stones, wooden decks, potted plants and the like. Views are thus "manufactured" in mini-jungles—and the light let in.

Kim Inglis

LEFT
Rooftop bathroom in a renovated shophouse in Singapore features running water and tropical plants to create a garden effect.

BOTTOM LEFT
Here, the use of natural materials, such as the wooden flooring *(at back)* and the stone *(at front)*, produce the effect of an open bathroom, even though it is fully enclosed.

RIGHT
One of the renovated bathrooms at the Oberoi, Legian, Bali. The addition of glass panels for security does not mar the "open" garden effect.

BELOW
A solarium effect is achieved through liberal use of glass panels in this modern house designed by Jimmy Lim in Kuala Lumpur, Malaysia.

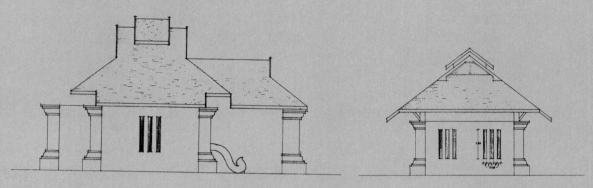

A PALATIAL SAUNA IN NORTHERN THAILAND

Visitors to the palatial home of Yvan Van Outrive and Wongvipa Devahastin na Ayudhya outside Chiang Mai in northern Thailand may notice that much of the lushly-planted estate has been inspired by Bali. On their many visits to the Indonesian island, the owners have acquired numerous works by Balinese wood and stone sculptors, which now adorn both buildings and garden, as well as a number of architectural concepts found in Balinese houses.

This is particularly true of the large sauna, which occupies a separate building and consists of several rooms. All the estate's villas have their own private bathrooms, but the sauna is open to all, as a health club would be in a hotel. Here, an elegant sea shell serves as a wash basin, while the wooden doors are ornately carved.

Perhaps the most Balinese feature of all is the outdoor shower just outside the steam room, where all that separates a bather from the outside world is a vine-covered trellis and some strategically-placed tropical foliage. This is no real inconvenience, however, since the entire compound has been designed to ensure ultimate privacy for both the owners and their guests.

William Warren

ABOVE
Beautiful glass doors in rich shades lead into the garden shower section of the sauna building.

FAR LEFT
Exterior view of the sauna building, surrounded by a well-tended garden. The landscaping took two years to design and plant.

LEFT
Looking into the sauna, from the outside garden: traditional Indonesian *mandi* bathrooms often have large urns full of water, as does this one here.

RIGHT
Dramatic mirror and sea-shell sink are eye-catching interior design features.

A RICE BARN FOR THE GUEST

"It's like sleeping in a fabulous adult tree-house.

There's something secretive about it—

you have the feeling that no-one

knows where you are..."

Diana Darling, author

Essentially an enclosed hut perched high on wooden posts, the rice barn looks primordially safe and snug—and it is this promise of lofty seclusion that inspires the thought that a rice barn would make an excellent "room of one's own."

Although it is too small to be a permanent home for any but the most ascetic Western house-holder, when it is restored and comfortably fitted out, a rice barn makes a guest house of charm.

Architecturally, the rice barn's form is a pure expression of its function, which is to keep rice dry and safe. Putting the granary on high posts does away with the need to build a watertight structure, and it provides better ventilation. In Bali, it is also appropriate that the abode of the rice goddess be stored above head-level. As to the fact it is enclosed, this is because rice is wealth and is therefore properly locked up.

Styles of rice barns naturally vary from place to place and bear locally distinguishing traits—an endless source of pleasure to rice-barn cognoscenti. Many rice barns, like those found in Thailand and north Bali, are built entirely of timber (even with wooden roof shingles) with finely carved detailing on the eaves and cornices. In densely-populated, deforested south Bali, the materials are usually bamboo and grass. Here the four-posted *jineng* and six-posted *lumbung* are basically roofs on stilts, with the thatched roofs of *alang-alang* curv-ing in a steep slope to the floor. The space below comprises a shady platform for working or sprawling.

The mutation of rice barns from granaries to granny flats reflects the changing economies of tropical Asian countries. Native strains of rice are increasingly stored on the cut stalks and threshed as domestic needs require, while high-yield strains are brought from the harvest field directly to a rice mill. Also, as the viability of subsistence farming dwindles in the face of rising land values, many rice farmers are con-verting their fields to other uses. In short, rice barns as granaries are gradually becoming obsolete.

The craze for rice barns as habitable antiques caught on very fast among developers of small hotels, especially in Bali, during the building boom of the 1980s. Neophyte entrepreneurs imitated the bulging "grass-roof-as-building" look for their new houses, hilariously pleased that such a cheap building could be attractive to tourists. The result was some-thing else entirely. These rice-barn style bungalows were conveniently bigger, but the proportions often suffered, and few developers could resist filling in the airy lower part with another guest room or two.

To use the rice-barn idiom well in new buildings is a tough design challenge. It requires an original building—dismantled, treated for pests, and often extensively revised (in the same type of wood), before

reassembling. It requires electrical wiring, plumbing and a certain amount of furniture sensitively designed and built in. At the end of the 20th century, expatriates no longer refer to their guest rice barn as a "habitable antique" but as a "culturally vulnerable, but protected, interactive environment".

Diana Darling

PREVIOUS PAGE
The rice-barn guest house at the property of Suchid and Diether von Boehm-Bezing outside Chiang Mai, northern Thailand. Set in a garden full of unusual plants, it has views over the Ping River.

ABOVE
A photograph from the 1950s showing a traditional rice barn or *lumbung* in Bali.

OPPOSITE
A Sumatran rice barn doubles up as a charming garden feature in the Linda Garland estate in the central lowlands of Nyuh Kuning, Bali *(see pages 176–177).*

A GUEST ROOM WITH A VIEW

Regarded almost as essential as the main family dwelling in a traditional northern Thai compound is a separate granary, where rice is stored for regular consumption as well as for planting in the next rainy season. Such a structure, usually sited near the main house, proclaims a degree of prosperity: according to a northern saying, a young man should take note of the size of his future wife's family granary. Also, when the granary is full, it promotes a feeling of security.

A granary is elevated from the ground on posts sufficiently high that a man standing on a loaded bullock cart can hand baskets of rice to another standing on the balcony. The rice is then poured inside through small windows. Unlike the walls of northern-style houses, which lean outward, those of a granary slope inward on the grounds that this made the building stronger and better able to bear the weight of the grain stored. The structure is also more lavishly decorated with wood-carvings than the main house, reflecting its significance in the family's fortunes.

Some old granaries are now being put to new uses. To serve as guest quarters on their Chiang Mai estate, Suchid and Diether von Boehm-Bezing acquired a fine example and erected it near their main house, with views of the garden and the Ping River. The building has an exceptionally fine carved gable depicting elephants, the elegant northern-style roof decorations known as *galae* and a balcony filled with pots of flowering plants.

William Warren

LEFT
The interior of the von Boehm-Bezing rice barn is decorated with Chinese furniture. Of particular note are the dressing table *(on left)* and the ornate bed.

ABOVE LEFT AND RIGHT
Two exterior views of the rice barn—the front facade and the long balcony running along its length.

RIGHT
Exterior view of the whole structure: guests not only have views of the unusual garden, they can see over to the Ping River and the rice fields beyond.

A BOOKISH DEN

There are four distinctive rice barns in the five-residence compound of Taman Mertasari in Sanur, South Bali. The traditional storage structures here are all true and original rice barns that were literally bought in the mountains of north Bali and moved piecemeal down to Sanur. Three of them serve as auxiliary cottages to the main residences and a fourth does comfortable duty as a communal library and tube-viewing room. This library *lumbung*—situated between the compound's main entry and the swimming pool—is the indoor heart of the compound. Here is where guests look for something to read or leave books to join the existing collection. Many of them leave copies of their own books, for Taman Merta-sari is a bookish place: three of the residents are publishers. Perhaps more importantly, the library *lumbung* is a place where people can gather to watch laser-disked movies.

The original pre-library *lumbung*, specifically called a *glebug*, comes from Buleleng on the north coast

of Bali. It is a fine example of the region's timber rice barns. Its exterior has, however, been entirely renovated, and subtly but sub-stantially revised, to meet the functions of its new life. The most conspicuous change is that the *lumbung* is set in a small lily pond-moat. This gives it a frame in the landscaping of the compound's park, and the evaporation of the water both cools the building and protects the timber joinery from fluctuating between the dry and rainy seasons. The lower platform has been taken away; stairs and a wooden deck lead to the entry, a pair of carved Balinese doors. The interior space is divided into the library proper, with a circular stair leading to a sleeping loft. Sliding louvred windows on all sides provide ventilation and allow the room to be darkened for screen viewing. The furniture is simple: built-in bookshelves and corner tables, and seating on cushions. A ceiling fan and refrigerator assure long hours of comfort.

Diana Darling and Leonard Lueras

OPPOSITE
This sleepy-time area is on the second floor of one of Taman Mertasari's three cottage *lumbungs*. One feels, given the shape of these structures, that one is sleeping in a chapel.

TOP
Louvred windows that can slide open allow for easy access to varying views of the compound's tropical garden and *(at top left)* the pool. A small stairwell doubles as an art wall *(front, facing)* and clothes closet *(behind the wall)*.

ABOVE
Exterior view of the library *lumbung*.

LEFT
Whimsically-carved hands at the bottom of the teak wood bannister lead guests upstairs to the bamboo and thatch sanctuary featured on opposite page.

ABOVE
Path leading to the
Francione *lumbung*.

BELOW
Light and airy bedrooms are
protected from tropical
elements with fine cotton
and mats of woven bamboo.

FUNCTIONALITY AND CHARACTER

Bali abounds in grizzled
rice barns, but few of them
manage to combine functionality
with the proportions and character
of the original. Gianni Francione's
double-*lumbung* guest house is a
remarkable exception. Francione
deals ingeniously with the
constraint of size by yoking two
lumbung with a staircase masked
by a wall of native stone. The rice
barn's height is reinterpreted by
setting the ground floor slightly
below ground level, creating a
central entrance and two shady
downstairs living spaces.

To the right of the entrance is a
sitting area; to the left, a dining
area and small kitchen. The half-
basement walls are screened by
thick planting next to the house.
This solution opens these quite
small spaces to the outdoors
without sacrificing privacy, and it
gives the downstairs area the
shifting light of an indoor garden.
Upstairs under the roofs are the
two bedrooms, joined by an airy
walkway above the bathroom. The
bedrooms are nest-like in their
snugness, with all the character
of a true *lumbung* and none of its
discomforts. Low, wide windows
at either end provide light and
ventilation.

Diana Darling

LUMBUNG AS PALAZZO

This private house is one in a complex of low-rise, grass-roofed buildings looking onto a swimming pool at Legian, Bali. A three-storey rice barn forms the main building. Its heavily thatched exterior is deceptively rustic: inside, all the surfaces are refined—polished marble floors and finely finished timber. The vast ground floor has a large sitting room, while a double staircase leads to a mezzanine floor above the sitting room. From this airy and pleasantly solid space, another stairway leads to a sleeping loft.

Diana Darling

TOP
The middle floor. The stained glass panel in the foreground sheathes a closet bathroom.

LEFT
The main house looking toward the ocean.

ABOVE
Heavily browed windows punctuate the sides of the rice-barn roof.

AL FRESCO LIVING

"Protection from the natural elements, the

sala, balé or pendopo can offer comfort,

tranquillity, conviviality."

Edward Tuttle, architect

Living in the tropics is all about relaxing, dining, entertaining—and even sleeping—outside. Because of this emphasis on the open air, many areas in Southeast Asia have produced particular structures that cater specifically to the outdoor experience.

One of the basic structures of traditional Balinese life is the *balé*, or pavilion. It might be an elegant *balé gade* in a wealthy *puri* or noble house, with a thatched

roof and beautifully carved pillars, frequently set in the middle of a pond for added coolness; or a *balé agung*, much larger, as often as not part of a temple, where village elders meet to discuss matters of importance; or a still larger *balé banjar*, the central gathering place for community events; or merely a very simple, basic *balé* in a family compound. In any case, it is always an airy structure, open on all sides and cool on even the hottest day, where people gather for almost their entire range of social life.

A similar feature found in Thailand is the *sala*, also open-sided and with the steep, sometimes multi-tiered roof and gracefully curving bargeboards that are characteristic of classic Thai architecture. Again, it is seen in a variety of settings, used for a variety of purposes. In a Buddhist *wat*, or temple complex, it may be the place where monks meet for their midday meals on a torrid day, or where pilgrims sleep on an overnight visit. *Salas* can be seen at regular intervals along the country's numerous rivers and canals, sometimes as places to disembark from boats, often as places to relax and enjoy the refreshing breezes that sweep along the water in the late afternoon, or as places for entertaining guests in private compounds.

Modern houses, too, often incorporate such pavilions into their design and use them for the al fresco pleasures that are such a

OPPOSITE
Photograph from 1910 showing a *sala* on the banks of a Thai *klong*. These structures were often used as the equivalent of the modern-day bus stop.

LEFT
A distinctive northern Thai roof is the principal design feature of this pavilion in the grounds of the Napa Doi estate near Chiang Mai, north Thailand. Traditional triangular Thai floor cushions comprise the seating arrangements.

PREVIOUS PAGE AND BELOW
Views of the exterior and interior of the classic Thai *sala* at the house of Marisa Viravaidya and Douglas Clayton in central Bangkok, Thailand. Even though the garden is fairly small, the *sala* creates extra space for sitting and relaxing on a cool evening. The rattan furniture is custom made by Pure Design, Bangkok.

feature of living in the tropics. One Bangkok house, for instance, has a garden *sala* with gleaming teak floors, furnished with silk cushions and low tables, surrounded by fragrant shrubs and trees that creates an atmosphere of serene privacy and effectively isolates it from the busy city just beyond tall, split bamboo walls. Others offer sweeping views of misty rivers, spectacular sea coasts, or rice fields stretching to hazy mountains. Similarly, classical Balinese *balés* (and their Javanese equivalents, the *pendopos*) have been adapted as places for outdoor dining with views of a jungle-like garden lit with lanterns or perhaps as outdoor theatres for musical performances.

Like the gazebos or pergolas of Western gardens, the *sala*, *balé* and *pendopo* are decorative in themselves, providing architectural focal points amidst the natural luxuriance of a tropical garden. At the same time, they serve a year-round practical purpose in the relaxed lifestyle of the tropics where so many social activities take place outside the house.
William Warren

TOP LEFT
A typical Balinese *balé* set in the middle of a lotus pond, positioned thus to catch the water-cooled evening breezes.

LEFT
One of the *balés* of a villa at the Batu Jimbar compound in Sanur, Bali. Constructed with giant bamboo from Jimbrana, and decorated with large white cushions *à la* Linda Garland, the *trompe l'oeil* painting on the wall repeats the ceiling motif.

ABOVE
Watercolour by Stephen Little showing the perched *balé* at the Von Büren house *(see pages 90–91)*. From this vantage point there are fabulous views over the Indian Ocean and to Java beyond. This type of four-posted *balé sakapat* is a simple construction, yet it is perfect for the climate and culture of Bali.

RIGHT
All the villas at the Oberoi hotel in Legian, Bali, have their own private *balés* or raised dining pavilions. Designed in 1970 by Peter Muller and incorporating many elements of vernacular architecture, the hotel set new standards for the luxury hotel market in Asia.

A SALA OVERLOOKING THE PING RIVER

The northern Thai home of Suchid and Diether von Boehm-Bezing is located just outside Chiang Mai, on the east bank of the tranquil Ping River. Originally used as an occasional holiday retreat, it has now become their permanent residence consisting of the main house, separate guest quarters and an extensive garden of plants collected from throughout the tropical world.

One of the most popular spots for relaxation in the von Boehm-Bezing house is an airy *sala* situated on the raised platform of the main building. Overlooking the river and

open on all sides to catch passing breezes, the structure is roofed with locally-made shingles of teakwood. At both ends of the room are graceful V-shaped features of carved wood called *galae*: the precise symbolism of these adornments, which are characteristic of traditional houses in the Chiang Mai area, is a subject of debate, but some authorities believe they may have represented a pair of buffalo horns to indicate the wealth of the family concerned.

The size of a traditional Thai *sala* is determined by how many posts there are around its perimeter. Simple structures have only four, while more elaborate ones may have 12 or more. The von Boehm-Bezing's *sala* has columns with carved roof supports made by local artisans who have long been noted for their skills. Furnishings consist of built-in seating benches along the open sides, positioned so as to catch the through breezes; these surround a low Thai-style coffee table, and one or two Southeast Asian ornaments complete the decorative scene. Of particular note is the 11th-century Javanese carved stone figure of a man comforting a weeping woman.

William Warren

OPPOSITE
The open-sided *sala* is the perfect place from which to admire the garden. The von Boehm-Bezings have collected many rare tropical plants during their frequent travels abroad.

ABOVE
The verandah, situated below the deck, features simple rustic furniture. It acts as a buffer zone between the garden and the house.

LEFT
An exterior view of the *sala*, as seen from the deck.

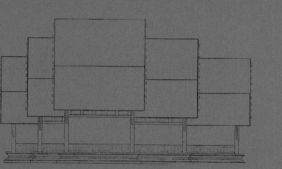

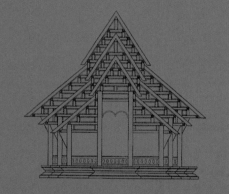

A SYBARITIC RETREAT

Sri Deva Giri, a sybaritic retreat recently created outside the northern Thai city of Chiang Mai, is a home that has taken several years to complete and that figured prominently in the owners' dreams long before that. It stands on a slight elevation that affords panoramic views of surrounding rice fields and distant mountains, convenient to a nearby golf course but seemingly remote from affairs of the world. The well-travelled owners, Yvan van Outrive and Wongvipa Devahastin na Ayudhya, have been inspired by a variety of architectural styles: several of the

OPPOSITE
Exterior of the *sala*: its height and proportions were determined after studying an old book on ancient temples in Chiang Mai.

ABOVE
A vase of heliconias in one of the guest *salas*.

LEFT
This old temple bell was acquired from an antique shop in Chiang Mai.

BELOW
Seating in the estate's massive *sala* is built-in, carved from stone and upholstered with hand-woven, natural-dyed fabrics.

OPPOSITE TOP
The owners found this Lanna temple gable ten years ago: it depicts a Hindu god eating the moon and symbolizes cosmic timelessness.

OPPOSITE BOTTOM
One of the carved *nagas* attached to the *sala* posts. Over the past ten years the owners have collected pairs of *nagas*, intending to use them as decoration one day.

ornate gateways and many of the art works displayed in the garden are Balinese, while the rooftops of several buildings have been adopted from those of Sipsongpanna in southern China. Other features are typical of Lanna Thai culture that predominated in the north until recent times.

The conceptual designer for the whole project was Lanfaa Devahastin

na Ayudhya. His attention to detail and meticulous research has resulted in some impressive structures, none more so than the huge *sala*. Recalling the design of classic Lanna temples which until the early 19th century were open-sided, it has a three-tiered roof of hand-made dark terracotta tiles and 18 massive red columns decorated with gold stencilled traditional designs. An old, elaborately carved temple

gable determined its generous proportions and a large bronze bell from the Ayutthaya period hangs at one end.

Other spacious *salas* are attached to guest houses on the property, each offering privacy as well as a view of the tropical garden landscaped by Surasak Hutasevee, and a stream that cascades through it.
William Warren

VILLA TIRTA AYU

Nestling in the foothills of Bali's towering Mount Agung, is Taman Tirta Gangga, the unique European-inspired formal water gardens, designed and built in the 1940s by the last Raja of Karangasem.

On my first visit there, I swam in the crystalline spring waters that gushed into the main pool through the mouth of a Balinese grotesque, and marvelled at the beauty of the setting. All the pools are fed from an ancient source enshrined in an adjacent temple. Little did I imagine, then, that two decades later I would spend a year transforming the Raja's former summer retreat into a small luxurious villa.

My aim for the restoration was to preserve the architectural integrity of the original style and scale of the pavilions, while creating flexible multi-functional living spaces suitable for casual al fresco tropical living. These spaces were achieved by opening up the main pavilion walls with pairs of external and internal sliding doors. When open, vistas are created through the two main axes of the compact site. When closed, they offer privacy and protection from tropical storms.

ABOVE
Exterior of Villa Tirta Ayu overlooking the formal water gardens of Tirta Gangga, Bali.

LEFT
The open sliding doors frame the vista from the bedroom. The screen printed canopy of Balinese motifs was specifically designed to enhance the room.

RIGHT
A perfect place to relax and enjoy the serene landscape. Rotan chaise designed by Carole Muller.

FAR RIGHT
The life-sized Vishnu statue reflected in the plunge pool was cast from unique teak moulds commissioned by the Raja in 1937.

ABOVE
The symmetrical columns
of the Raja's pavilion give
a formal impression and
visually link it to both the
verandah and main pavilion.

OPPOSITE TOP
A view of the entrance
to the intimate open
bathroom-court garden.

OPPOSITE BOTTOM
The balustrade of the
long verandah terrace is
dramatically accented by
rows of adeniums.

BACKGROUND MOTIF
One of the unique palace
motifs incorporated into the
villa are those on the non-
slip tiles used to pave all
wet areas.

The central focus of the villa is the
Raja's traditional pavilion. It is also
the meeting place for most shared
activities. Situated adjacent to the
pool, it is surrounded by a lotus
pond separating it from the main
pavilion and the moon-viewing
dining terrace.

Unique palace motifs are everywhere
incorporated into the villa design:
the life-sized Vishnu statues
representing the deity of the life-
preserving spring water, and the
tiles in the entrance court, cast *in
situ*, are two examples. In order to
reproduce the tiles in a special non-

slip, smaller-scale version, we sent
an original tile to Java to be cast
in a new metal mould. This mould
was returned to Bali—and the
"new" tiles produced at a local
factory. Imagine our excitement
when the first tile was pressed...

Finally, my dream was realized!
Working with local villagers and
artisans, together we created a
tropical atmosphere by uniting the
historical past with the elegance
and luxury of an international style.
And the villa still complements the
romantic vision of the late Raja.
Carole Muller

A SYMPHONY OF ECLECTICISM

This dining pavilion, surrounded by a lily moat, is a symphony of eclecticism. Styles and materials interplay to create an area where a mid-oriental hint merges with the tropical environment, to evoke a fascinating fable-like atmosphere. You could be in any fantasy-land— but in fact the house is in Legian in the south of Bali!

Eight white masonry columns support an octagonal thatched roof. The intricate wood fretwork, painted white, is Javanese, and forms a decorative perimetrical pelmet. The glass-topped table and black bamboo chairs provide the perfect foil for two antique Javanese consoles on either side of the pavilion.

Gianni Francione

LEFT
A magical area in which to wine and dine the hours away—it's a case of "Bali-hai" meets the Arabian nights in atmosphere.

ABOVE
Wherever one looks, there are views of the tropical garden and the lily pond surrounding the pavilion.

BELOW
View of the lily pond that surrounds this mid-oriental extravaganza.

BENEATH THE BANYAN TREE

Many people dream about having a dining room open to the tropical night skies. Madurese architect and designer Amir Rabik has one. Set against a tiered pavilion beneath a spreading banyan tree, this exotic al fresco dining terrace lends an indulgent touch to the natural beauty of a grassy cleft between Bali's hills around Ubud. A thoroughly expansive teak table seats six comfortably—but lends itself more to the kind of large, happy gatherings where friends and family eat, drink and make merry long into the night. Knowing Rabik's connection to some of the world's most renowned celebrities, it's not hard to imagine that this particular example of tropical dining decadence has seen its fair share of famous faces. Who might have sat around this very bench?

Well, that would be telling!

Nigel Simmonds

OPPOSITE
The al fresco terrace sits beneath a three-tiered home reminiscent of Bali's royal temple sites.

ABOVE
Open to the stars, Rabik's "dining room" personifies al fresco indulgence.

LEFT
The compound in the hills around Ubud is a playground of architectural and design exotica.

MYSTICAL ENERGY

This *joglo pendopo (see page 18)* is attached to a house that is situated at the foot of the sacred volcano, Gunung Merapi, just outside Yogyakarta on the island of Java. Transported from a village at the foot of a sacred cave known as Gua Cermai, the *pendopo* was reconstructed and adapted to fit the site.

The Javanese *joglo* is considered a sacred structure having its roots in temple form. Most Javanese would be hesitant about pulling down such a structure for fear of some kind of reprisal from spirit forces. When this particular *joglo* was dismantled the whole village came out to watch, expectantly waiting for some disaster to occur. Fortunately nothing happened: this may have been due to the ritual offerings presented to the spirits before deconstruction began, or it may have been pure luck. In any case, it now sits comfortably within a small garden—and acts as the perfect spot for relaxing.

David Wiles

A NOBLEMAN'S DWELLING

This *joglo pendopo* is one of the buildings in a traditional Javanese house compound near Yogyakarta which was originally a village headman's house.

Physically separate but connected by form, natural stone steps lead from the main house across a surrounding moat-style pond to the *pendopo*. It is a totally wall-free structure, and provides excellent shelter against the tropical heat and rain. In addition, the tall roof allows for the quick exit of hot air and gives the pavilion an airy feeling of spaciousness and elevation.

David Wiles

TOP LEFT
This view of the roof shows how the *pendopo* blends in with the other roofs of the traditional village houses. The connected roof to the right forms the garage—it also originates from a traditional village house called a *limasan*.

ABOVE LEFT
Constructed on raised footings, the *pendopo* has an elevated, detached feel and splendid views over the garden.

LEFT
The *pendopo* serves as a relaxing outdoor space with full access to cross breezes. The large teak columns and beams exude their own special aura and provide a vibrant atmosphere for social or ritual gatherings.

RIGHT TOP
The open-plan *pendopo* as seen from the verandah of the main house.

RIGHT MIDDLE
Rattan furniture and the *pendopo* posts complement each other perfectly in this spacious "interior".

RIGHT BOTTOM
The cooling pond and the warm colours from the high peaked clay-tiled roof create a peaceful ambience.

ABSOLUTELY AMAN!

Overlooking the blue waters of the Andaman Sea on the island of Phuket, the Amanpuri resort has acquired international renown for the luxury of its accommodations and the beauty of its Thai-style architecture. Ed Tuttle, architectural consultant responsible for design, formulated a resort where each of the guest rooms is a separate structure on a hill studded with coconut palms. Above the resort are a number of privately-owned villas in the same elegant style.

The classic open Thai *sala* with its distinctive curving bargeboards is a prominent feature throughout the Amanpuri complex. In the main reception area, this takes the form of a long multi-roofed wooden structure, dramatically lit by night, that opens on to a black-tiled swimming pool. At the villas and guest rooms, the *salas* may be relatively simple, with sweeping views of the sea below, or more elaborate affairs for open-air entertaining. Several, for instance, serve as dining areas with a round table in a sunken well and triangular cushions for comfortable lounging. Antique wood-carvings and old water jars add variety to the otherwise simple pavilions. Palm trees originally growing on the site were retained and rise gracefully above the terraces and pools.

William Warren

OPPOSITE
Each of the guest pavilions at the Amanpuri resort has a private *sala* overlooking the Andaman Sea. Architect, Ed Tuttle, says they were designed as spaces that perfectly integrate with the outside elements in a tropical setting.

ABOVE
Interior of one of the private villa *salas*: here the curtains have been lowered for extra privacy. Through the one open section can be seen a Khmer statue and a Burmese wooden door from the late Pagan period. Within the sala *(on left)* is a Buddha image.

RIGHT
Exterior of the same *sala*. Each private villa has two *salas* separated by a private swimming pool.

OVERLEAF
Drama by night. This *sala* features a sunken table, laid with a dinner setting.

"The spas and

pools of today's

landscape designers

are more and more

to do with

'lifestyle choice' and

less and less to do with

swimming."

Madé Wijaya, designer

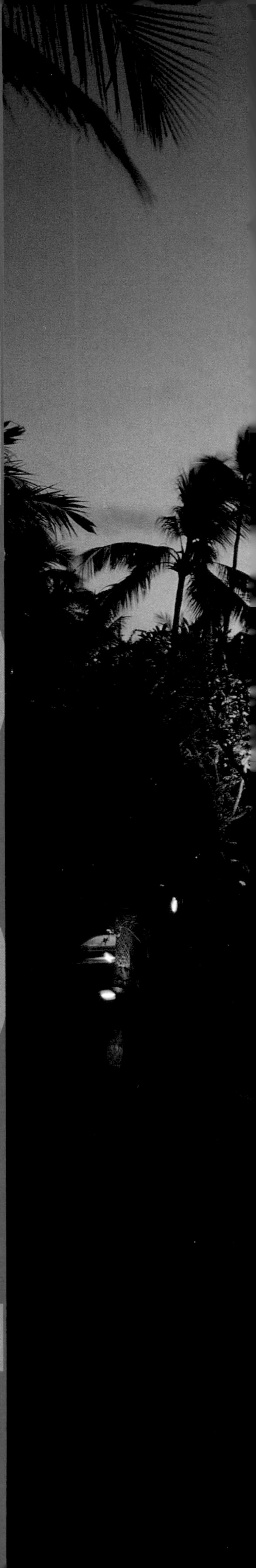

THE TROPICAL POOL

PREVIOUS PAGE
The swimming pool at the Bali Hyatt, Sanur, designed by Bill Bensley in 1985 when he was with Belt Collins, is the archetypal "Bali fantasy water garden". Carved gargoyles, caves and lush hanging foliage produce an effect of theatrical abundance.

OPPOSITE
A photograph taken in the 1950s by Luc Boucharge of Taman Ujung, Amlapura, east Bali. These classic Hindu-inspired water gardens complete with pagodas, pavilions and (unusually) a Dutch-style palace in the centre, were designed by the last Raja of Karangasem.

BELOW
The salt-water swimming pool overlooking the Andaman Sea on the estate of architect, M L Tridhosyuth Devakul in Phuket, Thailand. This pool incorporates natural boulders found on the site. All the surrounding stonework is fashioned by a skilled mason on the owner's staff.

Gliding above the shadows of palm trees on a tiled pool floor is one of the great sensory experiences of the tropics. Rockpool havens fringed with dripping ferns, gushing gargoyles and glistening grottoes are likewise part of the essential imagery.

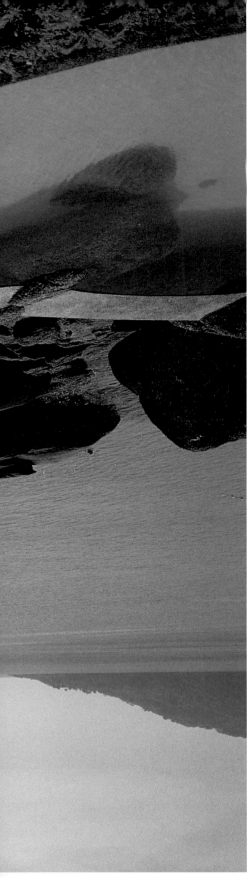

Charlie Chaplin's 1930s home movies of Walter Spies' spring-fed swimming pool, in the lush Campuan Valley near Ubud in Bali, was fodder for the wet dream-machine that produced the rockpool classics of the 1980s and 1990s *(see photos overleaf).*

But these modern-day lagoons had ancient counterparts. In the 19th century the Sultans of Java and the Rajas of Bali built water palaces loosely modelled on the formal gardens of their European counter-parts: Tirta Gangga in East Bali and Taman Narmada in West Lombok

In fact, Sultans' follies (staples in the great palaces of Java built from the 15th century onwards) were often water palaces or ruinscapes—and have provided inspiration for many of today's landscape designers. The royal baths of Taman Sari *(see overleaf)*, adjacent to Yogyakarta's Hamengkubuwono palace, inspired the pool at the Meridian Hotel in Jakarta, designed by Made Wijaya. Ruinscapes of the Indiana Jones variety have become a feature of many of the hotel gardens of landscape architect Bill Bensley. Architect Geoffrey Bawa's pools in the string of hotels he designed near Galle in Sri Lanka combine the South Indian reservoir tank look with trends from Acapulco, Hawaii and the Costa Esmerelda. Peter Muller's much copied classic at the

are the most gorgeous and most famous, though Taman Ujung, also in East Bali, *(see below)* is another example. Ruins survive in East Java, near Batu, of King Airlangga's forbidden baths, Jalatunda, built in Hindu classical style; these inspired the 11th-century royal baths at the Elephant cave (Goa Gajah) in Bedulu, central Bali, which, in turn, inspired Peter Muller's seminal "Balinese architectural" pool, with Hawaiian accents, at the Bali Oberoi in Legian.

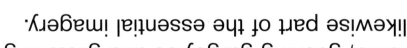

Amandari *(above)*, with its green slate tiles and limestone trim, is another pool design in this pan-Pacific-Hispanic tradition.

The idea of the tropical pool as a reflecting body-cum-water-garden (rather than an aqua tank in which to swim lengths) has taken root since the pioneering work of Bawa, Muller and Wijaya. The race is now on to produce the most exotic, most natural, most photogenic, longest, darkest, and most sybaritic, tropical pool! And of course, the resulting spas and pools are more and more a matter of "lifestyle choice" and less and less about the process of swimming.

Madé Wijaya

LEFT
A view of one of the pools at the Grand Hyatt hotel, Nusa Dua, Bali, designed by Tongg, Clarke and Mechler of Hawaii. Tropical foliage, an irregular shape and natural rocks are all incorporated in the design.

TOP
The pool at the Amandari, Sayan, near Ubud, Bali. Perched on the edge of a dramatic gorge, the *balé* which juts out over the pool doubles up as a stage for musicians.

ABOVE
The magical, mystical Taman Sari water palace, Yogyakarta, Java, as it originally appeared. Built as a Portuguese/Moorish folly by Hamengkubuwono I in 1765, today it is a maze of underground passageways, ruins and pools.

AN AZURE CUBE OF PERFECTION

Designer Ed Tuttle cut his teeth as an architect on the ravishingly photogenic Amanpuri, Phuket's most glamorous resort *(see pages 158–161)*. There, Tuttle exercised his twin passions for symmetry and classic Thai architecture with a showman's sense for spectacle.

The Amankila, overlooking the east coast of Bali, is the second of Tuttle's coastal Amans to be hung, architecturally, around a drop-dead poolscape. One thinks of Hedy Lamar and the heyday of "Holly-wood Hills gorgeous" when first experiencing the Amankila's cascading pool terrace and flanking *sala*-like pavilions. Tuttle's poolscapes are a joy to behold — and a joy to enter: for it is from

within the azure cube of perfection that one best experiences the stunning panorama of Indian Ocean coastline and the foothills of Mount Agung. Slung ever so sensuously off the three-tiered pools' sides are low-eaved pavilions called *balé sakepat*, with platform beds and futon mattresses in the Amankila gingham developed by Tuttle with

local textile designers Carl and Mirah Burman. These tent-like structures are romantic retreats for guests wanting private space or a poolside siesta. They are definitely Bali's answer to the Chateau Marmont pool chairs.

Tucked into the hill behind the formal swimming pool cascades,

Tuttle has created an elegant café reminiscent of the covered dining terraces in Portofino and Capri. His *pièce de resistance* café toilets are here realized in pure Palladian symmetry and coconut shell inlay.
Madé Wijaya

A SUPERNATURAL SETTING

The much-photographed Four Seasons Resort main pool in Jimbaran, Bali, was designed by Grounds Kent Architects. A pan-Pacific hybrid in the Acapulco category, the infinity-edge pool connects the pool plaza with Jimbaran Bay, the hills of West Bali and, on a still morn, the volcanic peaks of East Java on the horizon. This supernatural setting is enhanced by the architects' choice of celadon-green slate as pool tile and limestone pool deck. Madé Wijaya's landscape for the area was inspired by the backyard plantings in the neighbouring village of Pecatu—tight clumps of frangipani (*Plumeria obtusa*), pandanus and cactus trees. The lower poolscape by Madé Wijaya is a semi-natural rock pool fed by a seven-metre waterfall from the main pool above. Opera-box-like mini-terrace cold and hot spas are sexy additions to this poolscape that Wijaya calls "Jurassic pork" (for the bloated bellies afloat in the pre-historic setting)!

Artefacts from Indonesia's stone age dot the pool terraces. Scenic paths, fairy glens, bridal paths (for Japanese honeymooners) and the romantic site temple, redesigned by Grounds, Kent and Wijaya, complete the dreamscape.

Madé Wijaya

LEFT TOP AND BOTTOM
Clean lines and stunning views combine to create a poolscape of unusual beauty at Bali's Amankila resort, near Candi Dasa.

RIGHT
The poolscapes and gardens at the Four Seasons resort, at Jimbaran in Bali, were designed by Grounds Kent Architects and Madé Wijaya. *Above* is a photo of the main pool; *middle* shows the second main pool that is fed from the top pool; *on right* is one of the little jacuzzi pools scattered throughout the grounds.

AQUATIC CURVES

This property lies on the top of a hill in the Canggu area in Bali, and features an uninterrupted all-around rice-field view.

Its talented French designer has harmonized the curved shape of the swimming pool with a vernacular architectural style reminiscent of the traditional Borneo longhouse. Three conical thatched volumes each with a nine-metre diameter, housing the living area and two separate bedroom zones, are interconnected by single linear pitched roofs.

Internally, the elevation of the structure imparts a sense of grandeur without detracting from an overall perception of intimacy. The proportions are well-studied, and the result, striking.

Gianni Francione

LEFT
The swimming area has a semi-circular hot spa *(in foreground)* and a playpool behind. Set within a frame of colourful plants, lawns and natural sand-coloured stones surround the pools.

LEFT BOTTOM
Rear view of the house with its overhanging eaves.

BELOW
Internal view of the living area, set beneath one of the house's conical thatched roofs, supported by an octagonal wooden structure. An ancient Sumba *ikat* textile acts as a splendid backdrop to low sofas set around an antique Javanese tea-table.

RIGHT
One of the buildings at the Pelagus Rapids resort inspired by local longhouse architectural design, set against a backdrop of the tropical forest.

BELOW
Tranquil waters from a fresh-water stream feeds into the pool at the Damai Beach resort.

OPPOSITE
The irregular-shaped pool at Pelagus Rapids Resort features a double-headed *naga* dragon motif *(pictured at top)*.

"Designs of tropical pools are often irregular in shape. Lush landscaping and use of natural materials are paramount."

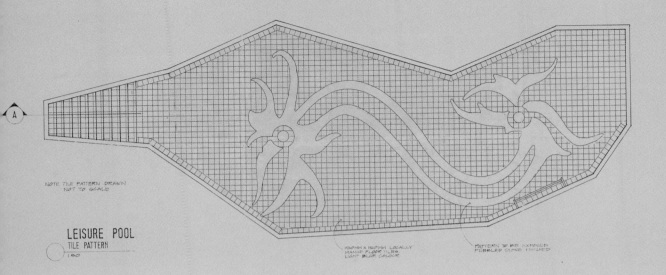

LEISURE POOL
TILE PATTERN

SARAWAK STYLE

Water features always provide a welcome balance of temperature in the hot, humid tropics. The two resorts in Sarawak featured here make full use of their pools. On the hill slopes of the Holiday Inn Damai Beach Sarawak, a hotel designed in 1993, palm trees and bougainvillea catch the sea breeze beneath the majestic Santubong mountains. A waterfall completes the ambience.

The slightly newer Pelagus Rapids Resort pool with its belian ironwood deck-surrounds is the epitome of tranquillity. Set on the banks of the treacherous rapids of the Rejang River, it is situated right in the middle of the rain forest. The ethnic double-headed *naga* or dragon motif on the pool floor creates a sense of mystery and underwater life.

Edric Ong

"This is really a garden with homes in the middle."

CASCADING POOLS

Few sites can challenge the view from Begawan Giri, which loosely translates as "Wise Man's Mountain". Perched atop a lofty spur on the banks of the Ayung River near Ubud, Bali, Hong Kong-based businessman Bradley Gardner has built a series of villas and suites that overlook a celestial panorama of tropical vegetation, rice field and deep-cut gorge. At its heart, a collection of tropical, spring-fed pools cascade down to the site's natural conclusion, the Ayung.

Started in 1989 as a holiday-home project, Gardner built his first bamboo house on the site with the help of local villagers and workmen. Soon his plans grew to incorporate a bamboo village—"the intention is to design environmentally friendly bamboo houses and give people an experience of living in them", he says—and today work progresses on more villas and suites. These follow grand themes—Water, Fire, Atmosphere and Earth—and will include such luxuries as baths carved from massive rocks and a fireplace surrounded by a spring-water pool. The landscaping has also been paramount at Begawan Giri, says Gardner, who "sat with the land" before planting more than 2,000 exotic trees. "This is really a garden," he says, "with homes in the middle."

Nigel Simmonds

LEFT
Water from a sacred spring feeds the naturally landscaped pools at Bradley Gardner's Begawan Giri.

ABOVE
As the pools throughout the resort are carved out of river rock, so will baths be carved out of huge rocks in some of the new planned villas and suites, currently under construction.

RIGHT
Gardner planted over 2,000 hardwood trees, excluding ferns and tropical palms, around the pools, in order to create an incredibly lush landscaping effect.

AN ENVIRONMENTALLY-CONSCIOUS ESTATE

Environmentalist Linda Garland's 30-acre estate in the central lowlands of Nyuh Kuning, Bali, is notable not for what she has done but for what she hasn't. A breezy open landscape that slopes down to a bubbling brook, Garland's style presents itself as a large-scale land sculpture, devoid of prominent buildings. Walk across the estate's expansive, grassy knoll—"there's a view of the river and an extraordinary *alang-alang* mound that looks like the cleavage of a giant Henry Moore woman," she says—and the visitor comes upon a dark pool that has been sculpted into the river bank.

The pool itself, like the rest of Garland's architectural creation, has made use of natural materials, its sides constructed from the same river stone that pebbles the stream beneath it. Fed by a natural freshwater spring, the pool is flushed by water from bamboo pipes and provides an inviting, 20-metre-long free-form pool in which to cool off.

Nigel Simmonds

LEFT
The free-form design of Linda Garland's spring-fed pool provides a natural focus to her estate and echoes its proximity to a sacred river. Its organic shape is more reminiscent of a natural creator than a renowned designer.

TOP
In this grand enclave of natural civilisation, Man has for once failed to monopolize the landscape. A bamboo protagonist and self-professed "Missionary for Mother Earth", Garland wouldn't have it any other way.

ABOVE
The verandah in one of the guest houses. The decor here comprises the signature Garland style of bamboo and sparkling white cottons, presenting a feel of tropical jungle living *par excellence*.

A NATURAL SWIMMING HOLE

If there were rules governing the design of tropical swimming pools—parameters for taste and functionality—then this one in Batu Jimbar, Bali, would fulfil them with ease. First, forget the straight line. A tropical pool should resemble a natural swimming hole. Second, banish the tile. Who needs the constant headache of regrouting? And thirdly, save the trees. The pool should be as much about the aesthetic of water within a landscape as it is about the act of swimming. We might also add a fourth category here, covering colour. The smooth finish of this pool outside Wantilan Lama, a breezy ocean-front Balinese vernacular home on the beach at Sanur, gives the water a slightly pale, sandy tinge—a more fitting aspect than the bright turquoise of conventional contemporaries. Designed by Bill Bensley in 1986 within parklands landscaped by Madé Wijaya and Ketut Marsa in 1979, the pool creates a quiet sense of calm in one of the island's most prestigious residential areas.

Nigel Simmonds

OPPOSITE
The pool is virtually hidden amid the dense foliage of a lush garden. A grotto hides behind a sheet of water created by a modest waterfall.

TOP
A guest pavilion on the grounds of Wantilan Lama is the original House "B", home to Kerry Hill during his tenure as resident architect for the Bali Hyatt in Sanur. Built by Palmer and Turner Architects of Hong Kong, it was revamped in 1986 by Madé Wijaya.

ABOVE
River boulders from the north of the island punctuate the pool's free-form design.

LEFT
The swimming pool at Tilton, Singapore, has been fenced off for security. It is accessed from an imposing semi-circular verandah.

BELOW
A view of the house from beyond the swimming pool. When the house was modernized, the verandahs (with the exception of the one seen here) were all enclosed in order to install air-conditioning throughout. Marble floors replaced the old wooden ones and false ceilings were inserted. The exterior, however, was left relatively intact.

RIGHT
A collection of palms surrounds the pool, which is set within a mature, well-tended garden.

A BOTANICAL SETTING

It is rare to find a mature garden in Singapore, one framed by fully grown trees, and kept in pristine condition. The one at Tilton, a late 19th-century house, is one such — and its swimming pool sits very snugly within this luxuriant setting.

The pool is a relatively recent addition. Positioned where a terrace once stood, it can be conveniently accessed from a verandah that runs along one side of the house. It is surrounded by a collection of 12 different species of palm, which provides both poolside shade and botanical interest.

The house itself has been thoroughly modernized, but still retains some of its original grandeur. A private drive sweeps up to a columned portico — and the front door. Step into an entrance hall, and the large living room is on the left. The verandah, featuring impressive stone columns and marble floors, is accessed from here — then it is only a step away to the pool.

Kim Inglis

OPPOSITE
The 15-metre swimming pool with two adjacent spa pools illustrates this house-owner's desire to provide the ultimate in recreational facilities to her guests.

RIGHT
Internal view of the central atrium which opens onto the pool. White concrete and wooden pillars support the traditional Balinese *alang-alang* roof, while polished ivory marble together with *palimanan* stone provide continuity with the outdoor paving around the pool area.

BELOW
View of the gardens from the jacuzzi, to a small *balé* and the sea beyond.

VENETIAN MOSAICS AND ADJACENT SPAS

In this villa in Legian, Bali, the pool area is definitely the focal point. It comprises a main 15-metre swimming pool tiled with imported Venetian mosaics, and two adjacent cold and hot spa pools.

A traditional *balé* built from an antique Javanese carved structure covers the hot spa and provides shade. Local materials have been used to pave the entire area. Sand-coloured *palimanan* stone slabs and light green pebbles provide a subtle play of tones that pleasantly contrast with the vibrant colours of the luxuriant surrounding garden.

Gianni Francione

THE TANG HOUSE

This house is a wonderful celebration of living in the tropics: Designed by architect Jimmy Lim, it cascades down the steep slope of a hill in Damansara Heights, a suburb of Kuala Lumpur. Its rooms are choreographed around a central staircase that rises through four floors. The stair is a "processional route" by which one experiences a variety of vistas, connections and enclosures carefully orchestrated beneath a soaring umbrella roof.

The steep slope upon which the house is sited has been used to advantage. The upper two levels are conventional in appearance, but the reverse is true of the other side of the house which opens out to views of the towering trees on the lower slopes of the hill. The living room projects out from the structure at the third storey level. It is unglazed and timber shutters can be thrown back on three sides. These external walls have an affinity with the permeability that one finds in a traditional Malay *kampong* house.

At the second-storey level, a narrow rectangular pool *(see right)*, which runs transversally across the axis of the house, is located at the base of the central staircase. The internal focus of activity, it is overlooked by the open-sided living area and the dining room from the floor above. Lower down the slope is a guest pavilion which has access to the pool deck. A small waterfall adds another dimension, the constant sound of running water soothing executive stress. The landscape around the pool perimeter integrates it into the surroundings.

Robert Powell

THAI STYLE MODERN

Not all tropical pools—and houses—are "ethnic" in style. This is amply demonstrated by this residence designed by Bangkok-based Architects 49. Located in the village of Nichada Thani, Nonthaburi province, Thailand, the house borrows elements of Thai design, but is starkly modern in terms of materials and detailing. A spacious terrace located on the second floor houses the pool *(above and right)*, centrally positioned to reflect the lights from the living room at night. The overall effect is as if the house itself is floating on water! A row of columns line the terrace periphery: they act as sentinels between the indoor and outdoor spaces, and succeed in effectively blurring the distinctions between the two.

Kim Inglis

OPPOSITE
The main feature of the
house is a magnificent
atrium space, capped by a
soaring roof structure.

LEFT
The pool opens out onto
a landscaped terrace which
overlooks a gully.

BELOW
The activities of the house
take place around the pool.

A SPLENDID ROOF

Many of the traditional house types of peninsular Malaysia and the Indonesian archipelago are distinguished by their splendid roofs. The Minangkabau house type is one example, the Toraja houses of Ujung Pandang would be another, and the chief's house at Bawomatulao in South Nias off the west coast of Sumatra yet another.

Malaysian architect, Jimmy Lim, recalls this tradition in his design of this house in a residential suburb of Kuala Lumpur. The roof dominates all the other features of the house. It soars above the swimming pool, which is located at the heart of the plan, with a series of overlapping layers. The robustly detailed structure is exposed to view. From afar, journeying along the main road from the city to Taman Tun Dr Ismail, the roof can be glimpsed hovering above the trees, like a huge bird. Sunlight angles through the gable ends and dances on the surface of the pool.
Robert Powell

A POOL WITH CHANGING MOODS

Located in Bangsar, a suburb of Kuala Lumpur, the Precima House designed by Jimmy Lim, presents a modest facade to Jalan Ara. Yet there is a duality in the house for upon passing through the main door a two-and-a-half-storey high open-to-sky living space is revealed which overlooks a sparkling blue pool. The transition is stunning. The living space opens directly onto the pool without intervening walls.

Two bedroom wings project from the main house on either side of the pool. These bedrooms and the adjoining bathrooms open directly onto the pool perimeter. Beyond the pool is a timber-floored sun deck and beneath the sun deck the hillside drops away precipitously. The house clings to the face of the hill with distant views of the city skyline and mist-shrouded forested hills beyond. The second storey of the house is accessed by a winding staircase to a guest suite, a library and a gallery which overlooks the living room and the pool.

The landscape-fringed pool is the focus of the house, visible from every room and vantage point. At different times of the day the mood of the pool changes: pale blue and luminous in the heat of the day, it darkens under an overcast sky and its surface becomes agitated in anticipation of a tropical storm. At night it takes on a romantic air as it reflects the lights of the house and candles on the sun deck. The effect is both calming and cooling.

Robert Powell

RIGHT TOP
Looking west from the second-storey gallery, over the pool towards the skyline of Kuala Lumpur.

RIGHT MIDDLE
The bedrooms open directly onto the pool, perfect for an invigorating plunge at dawn or a romantic dip in the moonlight!

RIGHT BELOW
Traditional dwellings in the Malay peninsular used high volume living spaces to create thermal comfort. The Precima House uses the same low-energy solution.

OPPOSITE
At night the house looks wonderfully romantic. Lights are reflected in the pool and the permeable construction of the walls—which allows the free flow of breezes—is revealed.

OVERLEAF
The sun rises over the house. The eaves project far beyond the walls of the house like a huge protective umbrella—and as the day unfolds, the blinds are raised to allow the natural breezes to cool the interior.

TROPICAL DECORATING

Indonesian Furniture

TOP LEFT
A traditional Madurese bed with characteristic intricately carved legs converted into a large sofa.

TOP RIGHT
A Javanese bed. The carving has a distinctly Chinese influence.

FAR LEFT
One of a pair, this 19th-century ornate gilt cabinet was inspired by Dutch furniture, reinterpreted for the tastes of the royal courts of Central Java.

LEFT
A *grobog* or chest used for storing important possessions and chair made from an old rice mill or *lumpang*.

ABOVE
This intricately carved teak wood and ratan sofa adds a regal touch to a formal living room.

LEFT
A rattan lazy bench with traditional Javanese carved headrest.

RIGHT
A mirrored beauty cabinet with strong Chinese influence from the island of Madura, just off the coast of Surabaya.

About ten years ago, the demand for original and reproduction Indonesian furniture increased enormously—and continues to increase apace. Today, there is a proliferation of it in furniture markets worldwide.

In fact, so-called "antique" furniture is actually between 30 and 90 years old, and can be classified into three genres. First is the "primitive style", the creation of village craftsmen: recognizable by its heavy appearance, simple carving work and an underworked appearance in the wood, it is rustic in style. Secondly, we have the Javanese style, which proliferated along the north coast and in East Java, close to the teak forests which provided an abundance of raw material. This furniture is more refined, with finer and more elaborate carving as seen in the *gebyok* or wall partitions of traditional houses,

wardrobes, tables, benches and a myriad other pieces. The third genre is the European style, largely influenced by the Dutch and English presence of the colonial times.

Nearly all this furniture is made of teak—a durable hardwood, easy to work and with a rich grain. The colour varies depending on the region, ranging from a light yellow to a rich dark brown. As the demand for these pieces grows, so has the production of copies in new teakwood or mahogany. Similarly, damaged pieces are often transformed into articles of different usage. For example, old four-poster beds are converted into lounges, rice mills become coffee-table feet and old farming implements adorn the walls of hotels and houses.

David Wiles

Thai Furniture

TOP
An ancient elephant howdah with ivory fittings.

ABOVE
A classic low Thai table, orginally used as an altar, from the collection of the Neold shop in Bangkok. Contemporary replicas have now become a common feature in Southeast Asian homes where they are used as coffee tables.

LEFT
A preaching chair, originally destined for an Abbot, has been upholstered with silk and transformed into a contemporary low armchair by Rama Art antique shop, Bangkok.

BELOW LEFT
Scripture cabinets, sometimes covered in lacquer to preserve them from ants and humidity, are now often used as decorative items. Replicas are popularly used to conceal television sets.

BELOW
A sofa made from an old wood carving by Jean Michel Beurdeley is upholstered in Thai silk in hot orange to parallel the attire of the Thai monk.

Traditionally, Thais ate, slept, and enjoyed social life on the floors of their houses. Therefore, furniture, for many years, tended to be only of the most basic type: a few storage containers made of bamboo, often lacquered for better protection, woven reed mats, some cushions to lounge against, and perhaps a cabinet to hold foodstuffs and a low table or two. These items gradually became more elaborate as lifestyles changed, especially in royal and aristocratic households. Tables, often of Chinese inspiration, had inwardly curving legs and beautiful decorations that were sometimes gilded, while larger, similarly shaped pieces served as beds. Even European furniture was often adapted to Thai habits, as in the case of a low dressing table raised just a foot or so from the floor, or, in the case of more conventional chairs, adorned with Thai designs. In contemporary homes, these are imaginatively combined with other items, many not originally intended for domestic use: a capacious elephant howdah, for example, which makes a handy seat or drinks bar; a splendidly ornate chair with back and arms in which priests sat to deliver sermons; or an old scripture cabinet, magnificently decorated with gold and black lacquer paintings. Whether new or antique, such pieces add a distinctively Thai flavour to any interior.

William Warren

Javanese Terracotta

Earthenware terracotta has traditionally been used in Java for centuries. Household utensils, roof tiles, as well as bowls for melting wax and large drying vats for the batik industry, are only some of the items that were regularly produced. Often this production was carried out in the home.

Today, however, the introduction of plastic, aluminium and iron have reduced terracotta's household use, although it is still an important roofing material. But, as incomes rise, so does the use of terracotta as decoration. The *klenting* (water carrier), *kendi* (drinking water storer), *gentong* (rice storage container) and so on, are finding their way out of the kitchen, and into the garden or onto a verandah. Here, they take on new roles—as plant pots or decoration—providing a touch of the ethnic in a tropical garden setting.

David Sinclair

ABOVE
Terracotta pots and figurines enliven this traditional verandah. The floor is also made from terracotta.

FIGURES ON LEFT
The art of terracotta production reached its peak during the Majapahit period, as can be seen by the examples of statues featured here. However, recent reproductions or new creations can achieve an equally good effect when weathered from a prolonged stay outdoors.

RIGHT AND FAR RIGHT
In the village of Kasongan near Yogyakarta, household utensils and water jars, as well as decorative items are still produced by traditional methods. Most terracotta is fired in the open using dried straw residue from the rice harvest as fuel.

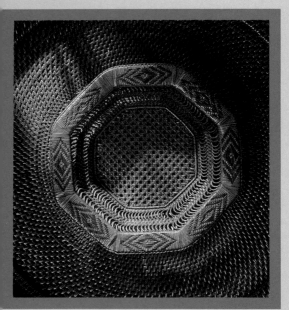

LEFT
Thai baskets from Nakorn Sri Thammarat can be used as trays or mats on a table.

RIGHT
Hand-made bird cages at the bird market in Yoygakarta, Java. Bird cages make excellent decorative items, with or without birds.

BELOW
Fine antique Bidaya baskets from Sarawak, photographed on the deck of a longhouse in Borneo.

OPPOSITE
In the back streets of Bangkok, young workers craft baskets in contemporary designs for export.

Basketware

"…it is now de rigeur to treat utilitarian baskets as decorative objects…"

TOP LEFT
The nomadic Penan of Borneo are credited with making some of the finest baskets in Asia. Their work can be acquired in Jakarta and Yogyakarta in the form of contemporary leather bags, as well as a variety of home furnishings.

BOTTOM LEFT
An assortment of baskets from Thailand. The large ones on the left are fish-traps used in the Central Plains; the smaller one in the front is a rice basket.

BELOW
Traditional duck-shaped fish-traps from Thailand. Historically used to store freshly caught fish, they can do well in a living room with an added glossy finish.

RIGHT
Thai villagers still make baskets for re-sale in their spare time between shifts of rice cultivation.

FAR BELOW
Iban baskets from Sarawak. The Dayak of Borneo traditionally employed a large variety of baskets which they made from every sort of natural material found in the jungle. However, as plastic arrives in this remote part of Malaysia, these skillful crafts are declining.

While some baskets are made to be decorative, and some basket-makers are recognized for their superior craftsmanship, most are simply utilitarian objects that serve a particular domestic or agricultural purpose. They may contain religious offerings, be used for rice serving and winnowing, for harvesting coffee, tea and vegetables or for trapping or storing fish or birds.

On today's interiors scene, however, it has now become *de rigeur* to treat these baskets as decorative objects—sometimes even as *objets d'art*. A general rule of thumb is the older the basket, the better: this has created a market for expensive "instant antiques" in the boutique shops in tourist areas. Baskets are easily "aged" by prolonged exposure to sun and rain, burial in the earth for a short period, or even by applications of shoe polish. Real antique baskets of the utilitarian variety are hard to come by as they disintegrate rapidly with hard use. However, baskets used even a few years will acquire a nice patina.

New baskets are quite inexpensive and are readily found at any open market. Local markets reflect local needs, tastes and materials, so baskets differ from region to region. Generally, though, the poorer the area, the more ornate the basketry.
Teresa Woods-Hunt

"Coloured pigments added to the lacquer allow the artisan to develop an intricate multi-coloured scene by etching through the many layers..."

Lacquerware

Chinese traders were responsible for the introduction of lacquerware into tropical Asia as early as the first century AD. Subsequently, each culture that adopted lacquerware transformed it to suit the local needs and aesthetic. In homes, it has found use as water vessels, plates, tables and eating utensils; in places of worship, it is invaluable as votive bowls, altars and magnificent Buddha images.

Burma (now known as the nation of Myanmar) has the largest and most diverse lacquer industry in the world. Dating back to the 11th century, it is believed that lacquerware made its way into Burma via the conquest of a southern neighbour. The present main production centres are located in Pagan, Kengtung and Kyaukka.

Lacquerware production begins with the tapping of the *thitsi* tree for its sap (*Melanorrhoea usitata*). This thick grey-brown sap turns black and hard when exposed to air and becomes known as lacquer. It is then mixed with ash to make a paste. After application to a framework of woven bamboo, it is placed underground to slowly dry. Many applications of pure lacquer follow, with repeated sandings being required to build a lustrous, smooth surface. Coloured pigments may be

The Chinese traders of Palembang, Sumatra, were very fond of lacquer objects and developed their own particular decorative idiom. Objects shown here include several betel box sets and various containers.

Lacquerware production has declined considerably in Southeast Asia, except in Burma, where it is still thriving. Here, families *(far right)* make goods even to other culture's designs, as shown in the Japanese-style boxes *(below right)*. A traditional Burmese plate is shown *(far right)*, while the items in the table setting *(below)* use Burmese colours in contemporary utilitarian and decorative items.

added to the lacquer: this allows the artisan to develop an intricate multi-coloured scene by etching through the many layers.

The recent opening up of Burma to increased trade and tourism has had a dramatic effect on the lacquer industry. Synthetic pigments and mechanical adaptations have greatly speeded up and increased output as demand has increased. Unfortunately in many instances the overall quality of the lacquerware has suffered. In reaction to this, large numbers of artisans have returned to their traditional methods and natural materials. They are also absorbing and adapting the new styles and designs which recent access to the international art scene has provided. The resulting lacquerware is of the highest quality with a beauty that complements interiors anywhere in the world.

Daniel Kahrs

"Lacquerware has a beauty that complements interiors
anywhere in the world."

Ikat

Weavings

The woven textiles of Southeast Asia are known generically as ikat, from the Malay word for "to tie" or "to bind". This refers to the technique of binding the threads before dyeing, in order to produce elaborate designs in the weave. Older, traditional ikat comes in a subtle variety of colours from natural dyes made from flowers, trees, roots, berries and even insects; newer and mass-produced ikats reflect the range of commercial dyes available, from bold neons to shy pastels. Old or new, ikat may be made of natural fibres such as cotton, linen or silk, or synthetic yarns—and each may take months to complete.

Ikat comes in all shapes and sizes, from items for daily use, to shawls, blankets and wall hangings used at ritual events and life-cycle festivities. Some are exchanged as a type of bride-price, some are used to wrap the sick or the vulnerable, especially during rites of passage such as tooth-filing, circumcision, birth, marriage or death. These ritual ikats are almost always made with the aid of special purifying rituals that ensure their magical or protective powers.

The myriad motifs and symbols woven into the ikat often express the daily lives of the women weavers, or the particular use for which a piece was intended. Human ancestor figures, ships of the dead, trees of life and so on represent the movement from life into death, and are often used for funeral cloths. The world of nature is reflected in representations of birds, horses and riders, deer, elephants, buffalo— which are often also seen as couriers of the human spirit to the afterlife. Fertility symbols, symbols of power, protective inscriptions in Arabic script, all can form part of the glorious kaleidoscope of colour and design that is ikat.

Teresa Woods-Hunt

ABOVE
A girl tying the threads prior to dyeing. The art of ikat, once widespread amongst the Lao people, including those living in Thailand, has recently been revived by the efforts of Queen Sirikit. Ikat can be hung on a wall, thrown across a favourite chair or used to curl up in while you dream of exotic destinations. Thinner pieces make delightful curtains, table runners or table cloths, and thicker pieces can be used as a unique throw rug.

OPPOSITE TOP FAR LEFT
Pua kumbu, the woven art of the Iban in Sarawak, is renowned for the finesse employed in tying the patterns. This pattern depicts a recording of a *Gawai Burong*, a festival which celebrates heroes and bravery.

OPPOSITE BOTTOM RIGHT
This Iban ikat depicts the Spirits of the Air; some are emphasized by being coloured with indigo dye.

OPPOSITE BOTTOM FAR LEFT
Lao ikats, called *mudmee*, usually come in sarong lengths. Because of their un-assuming patterns they are ideal for interior decorating.

OPPOSITE BOTTOM MIDDLE
Balinese ikats often feature *Wayang* figures and other mythical animals. This splendid example from Klungkung, showing a row of Garudas, is finished with gold brocade.

THIS PAGE
Ikats from the Indonesian islands of Roti and Sawu. Both examples incorporate western decorative elements, such as rosettes, into an ancient tribal pattern.

Indonesian Batik

"A classic image which brings an enduring elegance to any interior—complementing even the boldest colours and most complex textures…"

Batik's origins are ancient and widespread, and nobody is certain as to when it began. What is known, however, is that cotton from India, traded for spices, has been transformed by Indonesian craftsmen and women into dazzling works of wearable art for centuries. With the advent of the Industrial Revolution, when fine machine-woven cottons became more easily available and the copper stamp (*cap*) was introduced, production of batik began to expand significantly.

LEFT
Used to dress rich and poor alike (as well as the *Wayang Golek* puppets of Java), batik cloth is ubiquitous throughout Indonesia. It is now a popular medium for interior design too: batik cloth is ideal to dress up a settee on a verandah in the tropics, and scraps from old batiks can make fabulous curtains and cushion covers.

BELOW LEFT
The fabled *Mega Mendung* (Stormy Clouds) motif of Chinese influence is typical of Cirebon on the north coast of Java.

BELOW RIGHT
Tambalan (Patchwork) batiks, from the Central Javanese court, usually present a catalogue of the most popular motifs. This one here is typical of the genre, and is a pattern of great mystical significance.

BOTTOM
Previously, the Sultans of Yogyakarta and Surakarta ruled that certain batik motifs were to be reserved for the nobility. This *Ceplokan* with *Parang Rusak* background is one such motif—and is commonly known as a Forbidden Motif.

LEFT AND BELOW
The shop of Asmoro Damais in Jakarta caters to a clientele who still appreciate a kind of old-fashioned personalized service that is fast disappearing in the region.

BOTTOM
Stands, such as the one used here as an item of interior decoration, are used in Java to hold the piece of cloth while the design is being drawn. The cloth is usually kept steady by a weight attached to a hook.

RIGHT-HAND PAGE
CLOCKWISE FROM TOP LEFT
1. A *Sawung Galing* motif from the north coast of Java typically depicts birds, bouquets and butterflies.

2. This delicate motif—also from the north coast— reflects the Chinese influence in the region.

3. A contemporary piece destined as a cloth for a round table employs a colour scheme typical of central Java.

4. A Cirebon court motif features mythical animals and plants in a rock garden.

5. The dragon is an integral part of the symbolic systems of the north coast and Central Javanese motifs.

6. The Pekalongan motifs often feature geometric background motifs which may have been taken from decorative panels of ancient Javanese temples.

Batik is a deeply ritualistic medium: It is a method of resist dyeing, with the wax resist either drawn by hand or hand-stamped (with a *cap*—a copper stamp) on to a specially prepared length of cotton or silk. Tiny dots and lines of wax are drawn or stamped onto lengths of fabric, and then the fabric is submerged in a dye bath. While it is in the dye bath, the areas covered with the wax retain their original colour. The process is repeated for each separate colour in the design.

There are thousands of batik designs, with two distinct styles: These are the batiks of the courts of Surakarta and Yogyakarta and their surroundings, and the Pasisir batiks of the north coast of Java. The former are distinguished by a sombre palette of brown and indigo and abstract motifs. The latter is characterized by bright colours and naturalistic motifs; although both

styles originally used dyes produced from natural sources, these have increasingly been replaced by chemical dyes. Both bring with them complex symbolic systems once used to denote rank and to serve in ceremonial offerings.

The major location of factory produced batik is in Java in the coastal city of Pekalongan where commercially designed *cap* and hand batik are made for garments and items used for interior decoration.

Thai Terracotta

The use of terracotta for decoration, especially on Buddhist monuments, goes back in Thailand for many centuries. At the ancient city of Haripunchai in the north (now called Lamphun), early Mon artists used the medium to create beautifully expressive Buddha images and figures of disciples, as well as elaborate temple plaques and exquisitely-moulded votive tablets.

The art declined with the introduction of other materials but has been revived in recent years, especially by Suttipong and Maliwan Maiyun at a company called Ban Phor Liang Meun in Chiang Mai. They have created a variety of very striking pieces such as those used in the Sukhothai hotel in Bangkok. Some of these are rounded statues, usually of Hindu deities, while others are bas-reliefs depicting epic scenes inspired by those seen in stone on Khmer temples in Cambodia and Northeastern Thailand. With their interesting texture and soothing earth tones, which quickly take on an attractive patina when placed outside, these works have become popular features of both garden and interior decoration.

William Warren

FAR LEFT AND TOP RIGHT
Replicas of a pediment and a lintel of a Khmer temple, made of several very large plaques joined together. Here, they have been assembled in a garden setting.

LEFT
A praying figurine of a Deva, or a Thai deity.

BELOW
An assortment of fanciful and mythical animals decorate this garden deck of a mansion in Chiang Mai.

RIGHT
A pot holder of Khmer inspiration decorates the grounds of the Royal Garden Village resort in Hua Hin.

"The mystery and excitement of rediscovering an ancient city lost in the jungle can be recreated in your own garden..."

Thai Silk

TOP LEFT
Bobbins with a fabulous array of dyes.

LEFT
While traditional looms and weaving methods are still in use, what used to be a temporary home industry for women, has now become a modern industry. The largest centres of production, near Korat in Northeastern Thailand, belong to the Jim Thompson Thai Silk Co.

Undoubtedly the most famous of Thailand's many crafts is its lustrous, multi-coloured silk, now seen used in a wide variety of ways in both the fashion industry and home furnishings. Though little documentary evidence remains, sericulture was probably among the skills brought by the earliest Thais on their migrations down from southern China.

Certainly during the period when the kingdom was ruled by the great capital of Ayutthaya situated on the Chao Phraya River, it was a well-established art; the splendid silk costumes worn by a Thai embassy sent to the court of Louis XIV in 1686 created such a sensation that the patterns were soon being copied by French manufacturers. In later Bangkok, however, changing

fashion, together with a flood of cheaper imported textiles, led to a sharp decline in production. By the early years of the present century, the main weaving centres were in the remote north and northeastern regions, where only limited amounts were being made for local use.

It was, ironically, a *farang*, or Westerner, who is credited with

ABOVE
Checks are a traditional motif of men's clothing in Northeastern Thailand. They were immediately adopted by Jim Thompson when he first started ordering silk lengths from local cottage industries, and they remain a classic of tropical design today. This eclectic tropical interior includes a low table made of parts of a Burmese cradle, Javanese benches and Thai jars.

BELOW
A luxurious dining setting created with Thai silk of different textures and weights.

OPPOSITE
The atmosphere of an old time hunting lodge is recreated in this interior by Patrick Booth. Predominant is the use of a new range of jungle patterns from the Jim Thompson Thai Silk Co.

reviving this ancient industry. Arriving just a few days after the Second World War ended, an American named Jim Thompson was struck by the shimmering beauty of the few pieces he came across in Bangkok markets and decided, somewhat rashly, to see if he could find an export market for the material. He persuaded a few weavers to start working for him, gradually introducing such innovations as wider, faster looms and colour-fast chemical dyes to replace the conventional vegetable ones traditionally used.

Thanks in part to the wide publicity generated by the original production and movie of "The King and I", in which Thompson's silks were used for the major costumes, the material quickly acquired international recognition. By 1967, when Thompson mysteriously disappeared while on a holiday in Malaysia, there were hundreds of other companies producing silk and millions of yards were being exported annually.

Today, Thai silk can be found in a wide range of weights, from gossamer-thin to heavy, and an equally broad spectrum of colours and patterns. Eminent fashion designers like Pierre Balmain have used it in their collections, while interior decorators have employed it in draperies, upholstery, wall coverings, and other uses in countless homes around the world.

William Warren

"Thailand's lustrous, multi-coloured silk is used in a wide variety of ways—both in fashion and home furnishings..."

Celadon, a type of stoneware decorated with glazes, is characterized by various shades of green, grey, olive and green-blue. These colours are achieved by applying a layer of liquefied clay that contains a high proportion of iron to the object before glazing. The iron interacts with the glaze during firing and colours it.

Glazed Ceramics

The earliest celadons were produced in China, but Korea, Japan and Thailand are also famed for the quality of their celadons. Today, throughout Thailand, the production of celadons is widespread: ewers, dishes, bowls with lids and bottles with two small loop handles at the neck are common items. In some factories, traditional production methods are used; in others, ingenious replicas and other ceramics are produced using certain short-cut methods.

Kim Inglis

Jenggala Ceramics in Sanur, Bali, produces ceramic goods for sale in tourist shops and as bulk orders for hotels. Featured here are their famous lotus plates *(top left)*, a water cooler *(top right)* and *(below)* a mosquito coil pot, a lampstand and an ashtray in a tropical home setting.

ABOVE
Celadon pots produced by Mengrai Kilns in Chiang Mai, Thailand. This company produces various items using traditional methods. The pots in the background are a dull colour before glazing; those in the foreground sport a beautiful shade of delicate green.

RIGHT
Production techniques illustrated at the Mengrai Kilns.

TOP RIGHT
Dewi Saraswati, Goddess of the Arts, aswathe in moss and lichen. This image exhibits the soft embracing nature of an ornamental court, Bali-style.

TOP MIDDLE
Wayan Cemul, former gardener of Rudolf Bonnet, was a struggling artist before he was "discovered" by poet film-maker John Darling and later championed by the Southeast Asian landscape world. This whimsical head is a typical garden ornament in Cemul's signature "primitive modern" style.

BELOW AND BOTTOM RIGHT
Bruce Carpenter was one of the first art historians to collect precious Balinese stone art in the post-Donald Friend era. His house is alive with whimsical and wonderful garden art. The Nyuwun Jun holy water vat stand is often found in the family house temple of Balinese priests. A giant terracotta indigo-dipping vat filled with lotus plants is another great look pioneered by local garden artist and bamboo architect Putu Suarsa.

TOP FAR RIGHT
The crouched *barong macan* "tiger" carved into a soap-stone escarpment adjacent the Bidadari Spring that gave the Amandari its name. The arrival court at the Amandari has a copy of this statue realized by Nyoman Ketib of Kutri, Silakarang.

Balinese Garden Sculpture

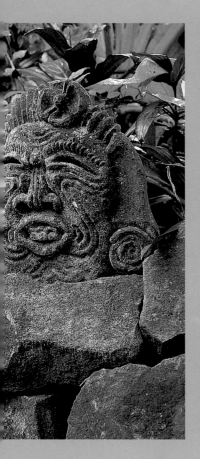

A Balinese courtyard garden is often "populated" with various ornaments: This is particularly true of temple courts which have beautiful shrines. Here, the attendant statues mingle with ornamental trees like the frangipani, croton and ixora.

In their courtyards (as opposed to their shrine courts for the gods) the Balinese suffice with the odd bird cage, pedestal pot or orchid stand. The expatriate community, however, are seemingly impervious to the inherited "spookiness" of these objects, and ornament with abandon. No dream home is complete without its Cemul-esque planter, moss- and fern-gathering goddess or demigod recently culled from a "village turned Christian"! It's all worth it though, for the joy a perfectly formed artefact brings to an herbaceous niche.

Madé Wijaya

The Contributors

Gianni Francione is an architect from Turin in north Italy. Over the last 20 years he has been based in Southeast Asia, mainly in Bali. He is inspired by tribal art and the vernacular architectural traditions of Indonesia.

Tim Street-Porter

Madé Wijaya (Michael White) has been writing on trends in tropical design since the 1970s. He grew up on a wide Victorian verandah in Bondi Junction, Sydney, and came of age on an open pavilion in Bali (for details please send a stamped self-addressed envelope to the "Relief from Bill Bensley Poolscapes Fund"). In his spare time he designs tropical dream homes and romantic gardens like the Amandari, The Four Seasons Resort, Jimbaran, Bali, and the Bali Hyatt in Sanur. His studio-home, the Villa Bebek in Sanur, has been widely published.

Robert Powell is the principal of RPA Planning and Urban Design Consultants. Formerly Associate Professor of Architecture at the National University of Singapore, he is an authority on the architecture of Southeast Asia. He has written several books including: *Innovative Architecture of Singapore* (1989), *Ken Yeang: Rethinking the Environmental Filter* (1990), *The Asian House* (1993), *Living Legacy* (1994), *The Tropical Asian House* (1996) and *Line Edge and Shade* (1997).

Julian Davison is the son of an architect and grew up in Singapore and Malaysia. He has a Ph.D in anthropology from the School of Oriental and African Studies, London, and has

conducted fieldwork amongst the Iban of Sarawak. He currently lives in Singapore where he is a freelance writer, illustrator, editor and *bonviveur*.

William Warren, an American who has lived in Thailand since 1960, is an author specializing in books on the culture and landscape of Southeast Asia. Among his many books are *The Tropical Garden* which portrays gardens in Southeast Asia and Hawaii, *Thai Garden Style*, a personal look at contemporary Thai gardens, and the best-selling *Thai Style*.

Madé Wijaya

Diana Darling was born in the United States in 1947 and worked in the theatre in New York before moving to Europe in 1973, where she worked as a sculptor in Carrara (Italy) and in Paris. She has lived in Bali since 1981, and began writing in 1988. Her first book—*The Painted Alphabet*—a novel based on a Balinese tale was published by Houghton Mifflin, New York, in 1992 to critical acclaim, and by Graywolf Press in 1994. She currently writes freelance and is working on a multi-media novel.

Editor and writer, **Kim Inglis**, specializes in books on the travel and tourism industry, and has a working knowledge of sustainable tourism. Projects have included *Beyond the Green Horizon: Principles for Sustainable Tourism* published by the World Wildlife Organization (1995) and numerous guidebooks in the *Eyewitness Travel Guide* series, by Dorling Kindersley, London.

Lawrence Blair spent ten years producing the Ring of Fire Indonesian adventure series for international television with his brother, Lorne Blair. Lorne was the architect, builder and owner

of the eccentrically individualistic house featured in "The Open Living Room". After his accidental death in 1995, Lawrence moved in and took over its completion.

Journalist and author **Nigel Simmonds** was born in Africa and educated in Malaysia and England. He has written on design, property and architecture for *Architectural Record, The Asian Wall Street Journal, Newsweek International* and the *South China Morning Post*. He is co-author of *Mimpi Manis*, a collection of stories from Bali, and *Banda: Islands of Fire and Spice*, a study of Indonesia's original spice islands. His first book, *Bali: Morning Of The World* (1997) is published by Periplus.

Bruce W Carpenter is a well-known author and a multi-faceted Indonesian art expert. He lives in Sanur with his talented wife Carola Vooges, who is a designer and artist, and two children Avalon and Allegra. Carpenter is currently working on several books including a major work on the first Western artist to visit the "Island of the Gods" and a catalogue about Rudolf Bonnet's collection of early Balinese modern paintings.

Carole Muller is an Australian anthropologist and architect. She divides her time between Bali and Australia, where she is currently renovating a boatshed loft in Sydney.

David Wiles, originally from Australia, has been living in Yogyakarta, Indonesia, for the past nine years. He has designed and built a number of houses both for his own family and friends. Attracted by what he terms "a strong spiritual energy" in both the form and natural materials used in the construction of traditional dwellings, he focuses on adapting these aspects in a practical way to suit a changing more modern lifestyle.

Leonard Lueras is a Bali-based writer-photographer-publisher who first came to Asia nearly 30 years ago. He lives in Sanur, on the south side of Bali, where from his home, Villa Intan at Taman Mertasari, he produces books, listens to the sound of waves and cares for his two teenage children, Lorca and Asia.

Architect and designer, **Edric Ong**, is president of the Society Atelier Sarawak, a voluntary organization which promotes the

cultural heritage of Sarawak and Malaysia. He has published a book on Iban ikat, *Pua Kumbu—Iban Weavings of Sarawak* and, more recently, wrote *Sarawak Style*, devoted to the cultural heritage of this multifaceted land.

Teresa Woods-Hunt is the Resident Director of the Council on International Educational Exchange's Indonesia semester abroad programme. She is an anthropologist from the University of Washington who has lived in Java for more than five years.

David Sinclair owns and runs a terracotta manufacturing and exporting company in Yogyakarta, Indonesia.

Daniel Kahrs is a landscape designer in Madison, Wisconsin, USA, when he is not fooling around Asia. He has assisted many writers, photographers and film-makers with their Asian projects, and has made over 100 trips into lacquerware-rich Myanmar since 1981.

Stephen Little lives in Bali and paints adventurous interior schemes using *trompe l'oeil*, special finishes and stencil. He also likes to sketch portraits. He provided many of the illustrations for this volume.

The "We Couldn't Have Done It Without You" Helpers

Mary Rossi is an Italian designer who designs and produces clothes for the export market. She has lived in Bali for over 20 years. Her extensive local knowledge and networking skills proved invaluable to the producers of this book.

Pino Confessa is an Italian actor of Commedia dell'Arte who has lived in Bali since 1980. Since 1982 he has acted as an adviser and teacher at the College of Indonesian Arts in the traditional Balinese dance and theatre department. He often plays comical characters in the traditional Balinese mask theatre and is also a classical Italian puppeteer.

Jeroen Aoys is Dutch by birth, but he has spent many years in Southeast Asia. One of his passions has always been interiors and interior design.

And special thanks to...

Luca Tettoni and the Publisher are grateful to the following, who kindly allowed us to photograph their houses and their collections:

In Thailand
Alberto Cassio
Anong Ulapathorn of Rama Art
Architects 49
Beth and Dick Balsamo
Bill Bensley
Chaiwut Tulayadhan of Neold Art Shop
Cherie Aung-khim of The Elephant House, Bangkok and Rangoon
Deborah Kramer
Diether and Suchid von Boehm-Bezing
Donald Gibson and Duangkamol Srisuksri at Mengrai Kilns
Ed Tuttle
Jean Michel and Patsi Beurdeley
Lanfaa Devahastin na Ayudhya
Marisa Viravaidhya and Douglas Clayton
Mom Luang Tridhosyuth Devakul
Suttipong and Maliwan Maiwun of Ban Phor Liang Meun's terracotta arts
William and Patrick Booth of the Jim Thomson Thai Silk Company
Yvan Van Outrive and Vongvipa Devahastin na Ayudhya

In Jakarta
Adji Damais
Asmoro Damais
Jaya Ibrahim
Mary-Jane and Mark Edelson
Ratina Moegiono

In Bandung
Daniel Meury
Dr Nugroho
Tan Tik Lam
Tan Tjiang Ay

In Yogyakarta
Warrick Purser

In Singapore
Didier and Marie Claude Millet
Gosta and Lisa Bjorkenstam
The British High Commission
The Botanical Gardens
The Regent, Singapore
The Shell Co
Woffles T L Wu
Yves Ogier of Corso Dé Fiori

In Malaysia
Jimmy Lim
Rolf W Schnyder

In Bali
Akhmad Yani
Albert Mantello
Amir Rabik
Bradley and Deborah Gardner
Brent Hesselyn
Ferruccio Fiorentini
Frank Morgan
Gianfranco Bocca
Giorgio Kauten
Helen and Rolf Von Büren
Julia Gaicak of the Four Seasons Hotel
Kamal K. Kaul of the Oberoi Hotel
Kate Moloney
Kathy Landis
Linda Garland
Marisa Curti
Mary Rossi
Mark Hediger of the Bali Hyatt Hotel
Peter Stettler of Hyatt Hotels
Rosy Marrone
Sophie Ehrenburg
Tim and Pauline Evill

In Hong Kong
Trina Dingler Ebert of Amanresorts